A MOTHER SPEAKS
FROM THE HEART...

What I discovered is that life, every minute of it, is beautiful and precious and exciting always . . . you taught me that along with so many other things in the weeks that followed —the most luminous weeks of my life.

I certainly knew always, as I know you knew, that we were not alone through all those unusual and difficult days. We were surrounded and supported with love . . .

"should bring . . . support and help in meeting crises that seem to have no explanation in a normal world."

—VIRGINIA KIRKUS

D1026929

The Story of Gabrielle

by Catherine Gabrielson

POPULAR LIBRARY • NEW YORK

WHEN DID IT BEGIN? When did the first tiny cell begin its wild multiplication to no purpose? Was it a good cell that had been corrupted into disobedience, or was it a seed of dissension and destruction in hiding from the beginning? When did it decide to break the rules, gather forces, and begin its savage and senseless rampage through your young and beautiful body?

You WERE nine that summer—a long-legged, sun-kissed little girl with long, straight, sun-bleached hair. You were strong and healthy, full of lively, irrepressible spirits. You had abundant energy and an extraordinary capacity to savor each day as though it were your first or last.

You were away at camp for a month for the first time, and we had the fun of receiving your letters, untidily scrawled and scribbled on scraps of paper but full of news and enthusiasm. After the second week you wrote, begging to stay an extra month.

But we couldn't afford to let you stay another month. Besides, with Deirdre in Maine and you in Wisconsin, Truro wasn't the same and I was getting lonesome. Four weeks without children was long enough for me.

The night you arrived back in Truro was a gala occasion. We had a guest for supper but no proper conversation was possible. You were so full of your new experiences, so bubbling over with the need to tell us everything at once, that we all just sat around and listened to you. Deirdre was eight then, and you promised her that she could come with you next time. You and a newly found friend were planning a Sisters' Cabin.

Together again, we spent the hazy, lazy days of August and early September wandering the beaches gathering our spindrift harvests of starfish and driftwood, of sand-blasted bottles, old corks, and shells. You were an excellent beachcomber with a sharp eye for the great potential in a broken barrel, a silvered log, yet never losing sight of the transient beauty everywhere that could not be carried home. The farthest reach of sand was never too far to walk when an unidentifiable shape beckoned tantalizingly on the sand horizon. Nor were you really disappointed when we came at last to a battered orange crate or a broken broom stuck in the sand.

By late September we were back in New York. Daddy left almost immediately for India on business, and you and Deirdre started school.

Walton was especially exciting now, because you were graduating into the Middle School and the fourth grade was preparing to go onto the Walton Plan. Your assignments were long and all the special teachers (art, shop, music) were from the Middle School staff and treated you like real grown-ups.

And you were growing up. You no longer talked about making midnight visits to constellations and you went to bed in proper nightgowns. We had grown accustomed to seeing you go to bed draped with colored scarves tied together here and there, for easy flight, I presume. They were absolutely necessary, you insisted, for your visits to the stars. You especially liked a trip you took frequently to the fourth star of the Milky Way.

But all this had stopped now and you wrote poems instead; poems that showed your inquiries were turning from outer space to yourself.

One of these was called "I Come From":

I come from foresty glade
From watery lake
From Mars, from the cold, cold moon
From the hot, hot sun
I come from hell
From heaven
From angels in the sky
From devils underground
I come from the middle of the earth
From the face of the earth
I come from space
From clear air
I come from the world!

Your reports from school had always been good, and Daddy and I were happy that the school seemed to understand and appreciate your many extravagant and divergent energies.

Even in second grade your report said:

—Fun-loving, happy and boisterous, Gabby is a very stimulating and outgoing member of the group. She finds enjoyment in all class activities, always suggesting ways of dramatizing reading material, etc.

—She uses creatively all the academic tools. Noisily she works on assignments and always finishes them in spite of much socializing.

—Miss Andreson (the art teacher) says that Gabby is one of the most amazing children she has ever seen in the studio. She has most of the qualities of a highly sensitive and mature artist, combined with an endless flow of energy and inventiveness. She refuses any suggestion, loves accidents in her work and is constantly experimenting but never losing sight of the standards she sets for herself in her pictures. She seems to work best in the midst of much distraction and chaos.

—Gabby adds color and exciting drama to our group experiences.

—Her use of colorful, imaginative words brightens up many discussions. It makes work more interesting for all of us.

Again in third grade another teacher wrote:

—Gabby is a most capable, enthusiastic and eager child with keen interests. She is a very dominating personality and always in the center of all activities. She has unusual ability to concentrate and can follow through all activities independently. She is showing great growth in her social development. She has outstanding ability to lead.

—Her work is all on a high standard of achievement. She loves learning and seeks new knowledge constantly. She takes part in all activities, carries through her responsibilities and works well with any group.

—In art, Gabby is still one of the most imaginative children Miss Andreson has ever known. Her energy, ideas, and facility with materials are beautifully coordinated and her interest and enthusiasm for painting are as great as ever.

—Gabby shows a real love of music. She has a lovely singing voice which she is apt to strain in her enthusiasm for singing.

—She uses her body with ease, imagination and control.

—Because Gabby is so efficient and capable there is danger of giving her more responsibility than she should be asked to take. We must remember she is still a little girl and should have all the fun that goes with this age.

I never told you this, but when I had my conference in the spring with your teacher, she said you were capable of going straight from the third to the sixth grade with no difficulty so far as the work was concerned. But, in every other way, you were right where you belonged, in the fourth grade.

You started piano lessons again with Miss Barzelle and loved the practicing. You were chosen to be the accompanist for the Middle School orchestra when they played "The Mighty Ship" at the special music evening in early December. You couldn't see over the piano to watch the orchestra so Miss Barzelle had to direct you from the side.

I'm glad I let you go trick-or-treating on Halloween even though it did get dark so early. Jane and Sue came over, and you dressed yourselves in odds and ends of costumes. You had sewn sequins and buttons all over my black-and-white summer skirt. Covered with old jewelry and glamorously made up, you were a trio of fetchingly precocious gypsies. We were all so indignant with that man in some apartment next door because he actually grabbed Susie and scolded her. He didn't have much sense of humor or Halloween, either.

Sociable as you were by nature, you seemed to want to be alone much more than usual during November. I wondered about this. I even mentioned it to your teacher. She suggested that it was probably a natural growth period—a period of consolidation perhaps. That seemed reasonable.

You spent many, many hours curled up in the cozy red chair in the living room reading. I guess you finally managed to buy or borrow all thirty-six books in the Wizard of Oz series. You said I ought to read them. I hope I'll get to it some day.

You started on the Arthur Ransome books about sailboating in England on the marshy inlets of the North Sea. You said that these books, which I think are especially well written, had an "interesting dullness." You were always looking up something in the *Book of Knowledge* and making notes. Your desk was full of scraps of paper scribbled with odd bits of biographical data or poems or quotations. You had notes on John Adams and his wife and Peter Stuyvesant and Patrick Henry. There was a folded paper with Patrick Henry's famous oration written on it: "Is life so dear . . ." On your own you started a research project which you called "New York's Names of Famous People." You did it going back and forth to school on the bus—The New Astor Laundry, The Pilgrim Bar, the Pocahontas Coal Co., and many others.

Such a miscellany of information you gathered. You explained to me once how cancer is treated with temporary radium, and you and Daddy had discussions about the structure of the atom and electronics.

Daddy got back from India early in December, bringing treasures for all of us—lovely saris, Indian bangle bracelets, sandalwood boxes. You were especially interested in the coins you found in his pockets. Later I found a drawing in your desk showing an Indian anna and its value in American currency.

December was damp and chilly. You complained several times about being cold in your old coat. I didn't pay much attention. I thought this was just because you wanted a storm coat like most of the girls in your class.

Lots of children had colds and there were viruses about, but you and Deirdre never missed a day of school. In fact, your attendance record at school for thee years was almost perfect. You had missed only the last few days of school in 1949 when you got the mumps. I remember Virginia saying to me early in December, "How do you ever keep your children so healthy? They never have even a cold. It's giving me an inferiority complex." It was true that we never even thought about sickness and none of us were ever sick.

Deirdre and you and I chose "Jeanette Isabella" for the new song we would learn for Christmas. Last year it was "Angels We Have Heard on High." You learned to play the melody, one hand, and you started learning "The Twelve Days of Christmas," one hand. We were planning to have a Christmas-Make-Things Club with Nina but we never got to it.

On the weekend before school closed for the Christmas holidays, you got sick. Not terribly sick, but you vomited once and had a tummy ache so I put you to bed. You had no temperature but you stayed in bed for the weekend. On Monday morning you announced that you were better, and off you went to school.

But I had an uneasy feeling about it, so at noon I decided to look in on you at school. Your class was having gym. You had been excused and were sitting in the little office off the gym doing homework. But your eyes told me how you felt, and you didn't protest when I suggested that you come home with me. We went downstairs together and got your things from the lockers and so, unknowingly, with no farewells, you left your beloved Walton for the last time.

At home you were tucked into bed and I phoned the doctor. It was most probably a virus, the doctor said. Orders were to keep you in bed and give you an aspirin every three hours.

You vomited once again the next day and once again the next. On the evening of the third day you woke at ten o'clock with a bad tummy ache. You said it also hurt to breathe. The pains got worse and you began to cry. This was most unusual for you and I quickly phoned the doctor. He suggested a codeine tablet. And, after an hour or so, the pains did go away.

We were certain you'd be fine by Christmas, but you were still vomiting once a day and I kept you in bed. You wanted to go upstairs to see Nina's Christmas tree. You said you'd never see it if you didn't see it before Christmas. And I said, "How silly, you can see it after Christmas." And you never saw it.

The doctor came once. But you were very animated while he was in the room and he said you were doing well. Just a virus. But, nevertheless, every other day, it seemed, you had another severe tummy ache.

One afternoon about four o'clock the pains began again and got steadily worse. You couldn't lie still and began to throw yourself about the room, over to Deirdre's bed and then back again onto yours.

You were sobbing and groaning now while I stood helplessly by. Then you turned to me suddenly. "No one in the world will be able to cure me of this," you said, "and I will die of this pain."

"What silly talk," I answered impatiently. And then, as the pains gradually subsided, I carefully explained to you that people don't die of pain.

Even though you still vomited once a day, you enjoyed eating and had no temperature. It was the recurrent tummy aches that seemed so odd.

You made Daddy's Christmas present in bed—four rectangular pieces of colored blotting paper tied together with ribbon and the months of a new calendar carefully pasted, three on a page. You knew exactly what you wanted for Deirdre, a little baby stuffed monkey like the one you had that she liked so much. Your present for me had been finished ahead of time in school as a shop project—a well-designed and sturdy dark blue rack to hold my belts. I have it on the back of my closet door and it's really very useful. I think it's the nicest thing you ever made in shop.

Deirdre and Daddy got our tree from the Associated Market, as usual. You weren't able to help much with the trimming. Nina and the Breckner children came and helped Deirdre. It began to look as though you wouldn't be up for Christmas after all. You hated missing the Christmas pageant at school on the Sunday before Christmas. The year before you had been in it, one of the third grade angels.

For Christmas Eve there were just the four of us with Nany. We had an early supper—you had yours in bed—and then we gathered around the tree. We had fixed a cozy place for you on the sofa, all bundled up with an eiderdown.

All those presents! There were beautiful new desks from Nany tied with red ribbons, and you and Deirdre were both terribly surprised to see the dolls—yours with the little black velvet beret and pink pinafore, and Deirdre's, an Alice in Wonderland doll with long white silk stockings. You both had decided before Christmas that you were too grown up for dolls. But I couldn't believe that. And there were white organdy party dresses, yours with a pale blue slip and long blue sash. You never got to wear it at all, except when it was too late.

There were too many presents, we all agreed, but I remember your saying "it was certainly the best Christmas Eve we ever had."

On Christmas morning you and Deirdre both got up early to see what treasures were in your stockings. You were feeling better and I let you stay up a little while to examine and re-examine all the new things.

It was then, in that early morning light on Christmas Day, that I noticed you looked strangely yellow. You were standing by the window, but I couldn't be sure. I called Daddy, and he said it wasn't my imagination. We put you back in bed and decided that we ought to call in another doctor.

So, we got in touch with Dave, an old friend and a staff doctor at General Hospital where you were born. We explained the situation and the casualness of our own doctor. We wanted the name of a good pediatrician. He said at once that we ought to have Dr. Lynde see you.

There was much telephoning back and forth. The turkey was in the oven, and we were expecting all of the Chasens for dinner. Heaven knows what plans Dr. Lynde had for Christmas Day, but by early afternoon he came.

You put on quite a performance, acting so chipper and casual and in such good spirits. I remember you asked him whether he had dandruff. That was mischievous of you because it was plain to see. But he was awfully nice, warm and friendly and careful in his examination. I told him about your severe tummy aches and he didn't seem surprised.

After the examination he explained to Daddy and me that you were definitely jaundiced, which is a symptom and not a disease. He said it was most probably a case of infectious hepatitis, an infection of the bile ducts leading from the liver. This infection stops up the bile ducts, preventing the bile from going on its normal course into the intestines, and then out of the body as part of the waste products. Instead the bile seeps through into the blood stream and the patient becomes yellow, and the stools usually clay-colored.

Although we had never heard much about it, Dr. Lynde explained that infectious hepatitis was very common among soldiers during the war, and, though it was not very serious, it often took a long time to clear up. He said that you should stay in bed, of course, and that you should have as little fat in your diet as possible. Because of the mildly infectious nature of infectious hepatitis he advised keeping other children away, adding that the rest of us would most probably get it, too.

Dr. Lynde phoned Dr. Brenton, our pediatrician, from our house and gave him his diagnosis. Dr. Brenton thanked him and then I talked with Dr. Brenton, and he asked me to keep in touch with him by phone—that it was most probably catarrhal jaundice—in any case, nothing to worry about. He was so certain that you couldn't be sick. You had never had anything but mumps, ever.

But he didn't come by to see you. New York doctors don't, I guess, unless you say, "PLEASE COME." Your condition stayed just about the same. You still vomited once a day and every couple of days you would get a tummy ache.

You hated the fat-free diet. It would have been fine for Deirdre because she hates butter and chocolate, for instance, but you delighted in hot buttered toast and bacon, and fried chicken and chocolate cake and pies. There were so many things you liked that you couldn't eat.

You sewed doll clothes in bed and sometimes we played games, but mostly you read for hours at a time. You didn't seem to have much pep but you weren't unhappy.

We began hearing all sorts of tales about infectious hepatitis. Aunt Teresa had had it and had to be in the hospital for four weeks. We heard about a whole family that had contracted infectious hepatitis, one after the other. It took almost a year for everyone to recover completely, and even then they had to be very careful about diet.

I used to sit on your bed and we'd discuss sickness in general and I told you all about how sick I had been at your age. And, with some sixth sense, I told you all about

my hospitalization for eight weeks when I was twelve
and explained in detail the hospital routine and you asked
questions. You said that in many books you had read
the heroine had had a long period of illness when she was
growing up. Somehow, all this helped you to accept the
situation.

I called the doctor every morning to report on your
condition. It did seem odd to us that you were still vomiting once a day, but Dr. Brenton reassured us constantly
and did not think you needed to be looked at.

But I was uneasy. You had been sick for almost three
weeks now, and your condition seemed exactly the same.
So one morning, I think it was the fourth of January, I
phoned the consulting doctor, Dr. Lynde. He said he
would stop by that afternoon and take a look at you.

You and I were home alone. About two o'clock you
began to have a tummy ache. It got steadily worse. I gave
you some codeine but it didn't seem to help at all. You
were writhing and whimpering with pain. Frantically, I
phoned the doctor to be told that he was on his way. As
I put the receiver down the buzzer rang. I ran to the door
and practically dragged the doctor down the hall to
your room. He tried to calm you down so that he could examine you but all he could determine was that your liver
was a little swollen. Quite suddenly then the pains began
to subside.

Back in the living room, he told me that you seemed
deranged to him. He said this sometimes happened in
liver disorders. I assured him that you weren't simulating
pain, and he agreed reluctantly but felt that your behavior
was very puzzling—puzzling enough to warrant hospitalization.

We went back to your room to discuss this with you.
You didn't seem particularly apprehensive about it. You
agreed with us that it seemed a good idea. People get

better more quickly in hospitals, we explained, and you were anxious to get back to school.

So it was decided that you should be admitted that very afternoon to the children's wing of General Hospital, one of the best children's medical centers in the world, and, incidentally, a part of the same hospital in which you were born.

DR. LYNDE phoned ahead and got you a semi-private room, which would come under the Blue Cross Hospitalization Plan and would permit visiting every day.

While you got dressed in your new brown jumper with the little brown-and-white checked blouse, I wrote a note for Daddy and Deirdre and left it on the kitchen table. We packed your bag and I put your new white wool scarf around your head, tying it under your chin. At the last minute I had to run upstairs to borrow cab fare from Virginia. Finally, we left the house. We found a cab easily enough and were soon spinning up the East Side Highway.

Now that the tummy ache had gone away, you didn't feel too badly. It was quite exciting, really, and, characteristically, you almost seemed to welcome this opportunity for new experience.

In the hospital reception hall I had to sign registration forms and waivers, and then the unsmiling desk matron told us to sit down and wait to be escorted to your room. It was only a few minutes but the delay seemed unnecessary. I was so afraid you would get another tummy ache sitting there. But you didn't, and soon a nurses' aid came along and took us up to the ninth floor and into your room.

It was a small room with just one bed. You got undressed and into the funny hospital pajamas, and Dr. Rhine, the resident doctor on duty, came in. The nurse weighed you and took your temperature which was normal. The doctor felt your tummy, and then he took me into his office and asked a lot of questions.

They said I could stay until bedtime that first day and that Daddy could come after work. Several pert, friendly nurses came in to say hello to you. A technician, who looked like a little girl herself, came in and pricked your finger to take a blood count. You didn't seem to mind it. She squeezed your finger and then put the rubber tube in her mouth and sucked the drop of blood up into the thermometerlike tube. You seemed quite interested in the proceedings.

The laboratories were closed over the weekends except in emergencies, and you were no emergency, so all of the tests to be done on you were scheduled for Monday. That made Sunday quite a pleasant day. We weren't allowed up to see you until visiting hours. They were very strict about that and we had to leave promptly at four thirty. But you seemed in very good spirits. We brought some pretty roses and Daddy brought the small white radio and fixed it up with an extension cord and we brought some books, of course. You complained about the food, but I didn't take that too seriously.

Sunday night at home a funny thing happened. Lynn phoned to ask about you, and then she said abruptly that her husband wanted to talk to me. Her husband is a heart specialist. I think he had met you once or twice. He got on the phone and I thought his voice seemed a little emotional, overdramatic. He asked a few questions about you and then he said, "I think your daughter is very ill, and I want you to let me call the best pediatrician in America into consultation tonight. He can see her at the hospital tomorrow. You mustn't delay at all."

It was very upsetting. I said, "How can we do that when we have every confidence that the doctor we have now is excellent. Gabby is in the hospital, the diagnosis of infectious hepatitis has been made, and a children's liver specialist is being called into consultation."

We thought he was an alarmist. He was instinctively quite right in assessing the seriousness of your condition. But we know now it wouldn't have made any difference even if we had taken his advice.

But that night I dreamed that you died. It was a very real dream—vivid, like an experience. A group of people were around me asking me, "How can you stand it?" and I replied, "I have to stand it because I have two children."

We knew that some tests were going to be made on Monday, but we didn't dream there would be so many. When I arrived at the hospital on Monday afternoon, you were full of indignation. First, they had postponed your breakfast and then, after promising, had forgotten to bring it altogether. This, on top of all the needles! They had taken blood from your arm twice, pricked your fingers again, and had given you an injection. At the end of the first week we tried to remember all the times a needle had pierced you somewhere. I remember we got up to seventeen that first week, before we lost count.

When I arrived on Tuesday afternoon, there was a sign on your door—White Gown Precaution. It had been decided quite definitely that you had infectious hepatitis, and no one could enter your room without putting on a white gown and washing his hands. I wasn't supposed to sit on the bed which annoyed us both, because it was the only way I could really cuddle you. We didn't always obey the rules.

You began to get all sorts of presents and that was fun. There were two or three weaving sets and puzzles and dolls and games and more books. People were wonderful. One day you got a big brown envelope with letters and pictures and poems from everyone in your class.

But the visiting hour was too short. We would just begin to make something, it seemed, and then it would be time for me to leave. The doctor had promised you would only be in the hospital a week or so, but he kept extending the time. He was waiting for some sign that the hepatitis was beginning to clear up. But your bilirubin count (the measure of bile in the blood) kept going up instead of going down. You didn't seem to have so many attacks of pain and they were never so severe. In fact, very much later, after your operation, you told me once that the pain had never been as bad as that attack of pain at home. It probably never seemed as bad because you had drugs to help in the hospital.

I decided to ask permission to stay with you through the dinner hour, and the doctor and head nurse readily agreed because they thought it might help you to eat more. You had practically stopped eating altogether.

And then I found out about the food. The nurse had said that you often cried when she brought your meals and occasionally even vomited. But it was so understandable.

To begin with, you were on a bland, fat-free diet planned, apparently, for young children. It was baby food, just like you said. Mashed and sometimes strained vegetables, meat without seasoning, and very little variety in the menu. The portions were large, unattractively served, usually cold, and nearly always tasteless. For instance, you had slightly cold boiled carrots for supper three nights in a row. And you were so hungry. When you took the lid off the dishes your eyes would fill with tears.

But we did solve that problem somewhat. With the doctor's tacit approval we worked out a way of bringing food into the hospital. Daddy and I went shopping for a large insulated container and a set of oven-proof dishes to fit inside. All this fitted into a square cardboard box which I carried into the hospital at visiting hour time every day.

It was fun fixing things that you really liked to eat— escalloped potatoes, meat loaf, broiled steak and onions, beef stew with tomatoes. I made gelatin salads with shaved carrots, olives, fresh peas—and you so loved the eating. You actually began to gain weight, ever so little, even up to the week of your operation.

It's strange that the tummy aches you had in the hospital didn't seem to be so severe. I remember one attack though. We rang the bell and were waiting for a sedative when one of the nurses in charge of the floor walked in. She laughed at you. Your braids were all undone and your face was contorted with pain. "What's the matter, Gabby?" she laughed. "You look like something out of the snake pit."

Whether she thought you would get the reference to an insane asylum or just connect it with snakes, I don't know. But it seemed a very stupid thing to say to a child. But I guess nurses can't always be thoughtful and on the whole they were nice.

You were still very yellow, which wasn't at all unattractive. With your wide-apart eyes, it made you look like a little Japanese girl with blonde hair. Every morning the doctor had you look toward the window, and in the bright morning light he would try to assess the amount of bile in the blood. And every Monday the bilirubin count was taken officially with a blood test. When you were admitted the count was twelve. The assumption was that it would gradually lessen, but by the time of your operation it had gone up to seventeen. But it's funny that at the beginning of April it had dropped to twelve again.

Because the doctor had promised you would only be in the hospital a week or so, every extension of a day was a real disappointment. I saw Dr. Klion, the liver specialist, and Dr. Lynde almost every afternoon. They were beginning to be a little puzzled that the bilirubin count wasn't subsiding, but, on the other hand, clinically you seemed quite well. You weren't vomiting quite so often, your appetite was good, you were maintaining your weight, even gaining a tiny bit.

But one day Dr. Lynde told me they had decided to bring your case before the staff conference—a weekly meeting of resident and staff doctors in which interesting and puzzling cases were presented, often in person. Afterward you told me about this. You were wheeled in to a conference of all the staff doctors and the young resident, Dr. Heldt, summarized your case. He held your hand, you said, and they asked you questions. I heard later that you were very poised and gave very grown-up answers.

Dr. Heldt told me that in reporting your case the chart said, "The mother reports severe pain at home, though this has not been observed in the hospital." No one really believed the pain. But after the conference, all sorts of doctors came up to read your chart and drop in on you. This was during the time when you had the walls of your room covered with all the different-shaped balloons that Babette sent you, placed on the walls with blanket friction. The doctors all seemed to enjoy the balloons and you didn't seem to mind all the attention, but Daddy and I began to realize that there were many different opinions among the doctors about what was wrong with you.

New tests were being made all the time. You kept your own fluid chart, and you were very conscientious about marking down exactly how much liquid you drank, trying to drink as much as possible. You were so co-operative, even the time they put the tube down your nose into your tummy and kept it there for three or four hours, the nurse patiently trying to bring up some of the fluid around the opening of the bile ducts to test it. The tube had to be put in place under the fluoroscope and then it shifted, and you and the nurse had to go downstairs again to readjust it under the fluoroscope. You were very cheerful about all this even though you missed your lunch. When I arrived for visiting hours in the afternoon, you still had that tube in your nose and you made us all laugh by saying, "You know I hate peanut butter, but what I'd really like right now is a peanut butter sandwich." The thought of trying to swallow peanut butter with that tube was too funny.

One afternoon we were sitting quietly and you said, suddenly, "Oh, Mummy, I feel so funny. I feel so strange."

"It's probably just another tummy ache coming," I said, "I'll lift you out of bed and maybe it'll go away." And I did lift you out of bed and onto my lap. You didn't seem to be having any pains, but you looked very strangely at me.

"I feel the same but very different," you said. I didn't know what to say. "Well, I'm sure if it's a little pain, it will go away in a few minutes."

And then you turned to me and said very emphatically, "You don't understand. It isn't physical. It's very important, I wonder what it means."

I felt very stupid and quite at a loss. "Perhaps God has just given you some extra energy," I offered lamely, in explanation.

When Daddy came from work a few minutes later, you told him happily that you had just had a wonderful experience—God had given you some energy.

During your fourth week in the hospital, Dr. Lynde began to talk about the possibility of an exploratory operation. Some of the staff doctors thought it should be done right away, but Dr. Lynde was not so sure. If you did have infectious hepatitis, as diagnosed, the operation might be a little dangerous. Besides, in liver disorders anesthetics are sometimes not absorbed so well. Dr. Lynde was cautious.

The senior liver specialist of the adult division of the hospital was called into consultation. I was told that he had seen more cases of liver disorders than any man in the United States. After going over your records and examining you, he took me into the hall. We sat on the bench in the corridor and he advised me against the operation.

"If it were my child," he said, "I would wait another week." And then he told me about a case of infectious hepatitis several years ago that was very similar to yours and took just as long as yours was taking to clear up.

But the decision was up to Dr. Lynde. Together with Dr. Klion, the children's liver specialist, he did tell us one day during that fourth week that there was the possibility of a small tumor somewhere. But nothing to worry about, Dr. Klion assured us.

It was decided to take X rays again. The X rays showed nothing except a very slight narrowing of the duodenum, most probably caused by peristaltic action. But the very careful chief of the X-ray department ordered the X rays taken again.

"It's nothing," several doctors assured me. "We read the X rays, too, and they show nothing." But this time the same narrowing showed up in the same place and, in addition, this X ray had incidentally taken in part of the stomach, showing a dark, shadowy indentation.

Dr. Lynde ordered the operation for Saturday morning. You were upset and began to cry when we told you.

You had expected to be going home, and I had to remind you that I expected you to be very brave, just as, later on, you had to remind me.

But then, in your reasonable way, you agreed with us that it would be better to find the cause of your misbehaving liver and get it over with.

WEDNESDAY afternoon you had a blood transfusion, your second, in preparation for the operation. You didn't like the idea of the blood very much even though it did look quite beautiful, like a jar of cranberry juice, we said. The name of the donor was on the jar, Andy Marks, which sort of made you Mrs. Andy Marks, the nurse joked. The resident doctor, Dr. Heldt, told you that you shouldn't mind the blood because little Julie across the hall got a transfusion every day and she was only seven. What he didn't tell you was that Julie had aplastic anemia.

In the middle of the transfusion you suddenly got chills. I rang for Miss Giffen, the nurse, and that was the end of that transfusion. She pulled out the needle and we bundled you with hot blankets and gave you some hot tea. Miss Giffen explained that it wasn't unusual. Andy Marks' blood just wasn't quite right for you.

By Friday you were quite reconciled to the operation. I managed to find *Coot Club*, the Arthur Ransome book you wanted, and brought it to the hospital. You seemed in excellent spirits but on Friday afternoon for the first time you had a bloody stool. I showed the nurse and the floor doctor. You also vomited once and the vomitus was red. You saw my alarmed look and were so quick to reassure me. "Don't worry about that, Mimsy, I had beets for lunch." Did you really have beets for lunch?

Dr. Lynde told me a little about the surgeon he had selected for the operation and arranged for us to meet him late on Friday afternoon. He seemed nice enough but awfully serious and gloomy. He told us it would be a difficult operation. "In fact," he added, "it'll be touch and go." Touch and go? "Oh, I don't mean to alarm you," he said as I broke away. "Everything will go all right, but of course, we don't know what we'll find." He had already heard about the bleeding.

"It's just his way," the resident doctor and nurses told me. "It doesn't mean a thing."

Daddy and I both stayed with you that evening. You were to go to the operating room first thing in the morning and we weren't allowed to see you before—against the rules. You were to be wakened at six for a blood transfusion before going to the operating room. Dr. Heldt, the resident doctor you loved so much, told me afterward that on the morning of your operation when he was getting your transfusion ready, he decided to prepare you a little for the operation. As he was carefully explaining things, he looked down at you and you had an amused smile on your face. "Why are you telling me all those things that way?" you said. "I'm not afraid."

He said he felt sort of silly. He said he had talked to the chief doctor of the hospital about you, saying that in his brief experience in medicine he had never met a better patient, adult or child, or one with such a serene attitude toward illness.

Daddy and I left about eight thirty, saying we would see you after the operation. But in the elevator, we met Dr. Lynde who said he was going up to do a biopsy on you.

"Just a precaution," he said, "in preparation for the operation." If there should be a malignant tumor, it would be helpful to know before the operation.

"By taking some blood from the spinal bone marrow and examining it microscopically," he went on, "malignancy can often be detected."

He said it was a simple little operation, that it would only take a few minutes, and we could, of course, see you afterward.

We waited downstairs, Daddy and I, unable even to talk to each other, our thoughts tumbling through our heads—biopsy, malignancy, tumors—what did it all mean?

You were just snuggling down "to have a good read before going to sleep," as you told us later, when they came and took you to the treatment room. I thought this would upset you, but when we came into your room a few minutes later, you were busily chatting with the nurse, not at all upset. You said it didn't hurt a bit; you were in such high spirits.

We kissed you good night all over again. I listened to your prayers while Daddy waited in the hall. The last kiss—I had turned out the light and had reached the door, when you stopped me.

"You know, Mummy, I can bear anything," you said.

"Uh-huh," I mumbled at the door.

"Except maybe torture but there isn't anything like that any more. You know, Mummy," you went on, "even if a person were dying of cancer, he could bear it. He would just go to heaven afterward anyway."

I couldn't think of anything to say. I just shut the door softly and stepped into the hall. Daddy was waiting there and I repeated your words to him. We drove home, preoccupied.

Next morning we were back at the hospital at nine. Dr. Lynde said the actual operation would start about eight thirty. We waited in the large waiting room near the doctors' private offices for a while. Mothers were coming in with babies and little children for checkups. Then, I don't remember why, we moved into one of the little waiting rooms near the main elevators. It was there Dr. Lynde found us about ten o'clock. He came in, pale and shaken, smoking a cigarette.

"It's worse than our worst fears," he said. "We found a tumor that has grown out from the spine in muscle tissue, invading everything. The whole area of the pancreas is involved, the liver—there are two or three ulcers in the stomach which Dr. Ferrone is removing, maybe more that he can't get at. We're almost certain that it's malignant—a preliminary examination shows that—but, of course, we'll have to wait for a detailed examination of the tissue. There's nothing we can do. We couldn't begin to remove it. Believe me," he added lamely, "I think I feel almost as badly as you."

I don't remember what happened next. A thousand years went by.

"But surely it can be treated," we begged. "Radium, new drugs, surely——"

But the kind and just doctor did not hold out the proverbial shred of hope.

"If it's the kind of tumor we suspect, it does not respond at all to radiotherapy. There are no drugs that benefit this kind of cancer."

One of our first reactions was strange. "Then couldn't she die now, during the operation? She was so happy last night, so fearless—then she would never know."

"There's nothing I can do about that. She seems to be standing the operation very well. Of course, anything can happen any minute."

"But the pain," we begged.

"I think I can guarantee that I can control the pain," the doctor promised.

What wrong thinking that was on our part, darling. What I discovered later is that life, every minute of it, is beautiful and precious and exciting always, no matter what the condition of the body. You taught me that along with so many other things in the weeks that followed—the most luminous weeks of my life.

I quickly phoned two friends—special friends, unknown to each other, who I thought might be able to help you. I don't know whether either of them ever goes inside a church, but I do know they live close to God, dedicated, and are sometimes able to direct light into dark places.

And then we had to phone Nany. She was waiting at home and we were to phone her the minute we knew the outcome of the operation. We told her that the operation had gone well. A few ulcers were removed from your stomach. You would be fine.

We went up to the ninth floor. You were brought up almost at once and wheeled into your room, still under anesthesia. The surgeon, Dr. Ferrone, came to us in the little ninth floor waiting room, shaking his head. "I did what I could. I've never seen anything like it—fantastic. Why don't you both go home and get some rest? She won't be conscious for hours." (You were, though, a short time later.)

Our old friend Dave came in. He was the one who had recommended that we switch doctors back in December, the one who had suggested Dr. Lynde. He had been at the operation, too, along with many others. Suddenly, as a matter of fact, everyone had turned to him. It was a cancer and he was one of the chief radiologists at the hospital.

"I had them put in silver clips to mark off the largest area, just in case," he said, "but we're pretty certain this is a kind of tumor which doesn't respond at all to radiological treatment. It has invaded such a large area that it must have been growing for months and months. We know of nothing we can do. There is no way of predicting the course of the disease. We don't know how long Gabby can live. It may be a matter of weeks or months. We don't know. We don't know.

"My advice," he went on, "is to tell no one. It'll be easier for you and easier for Gabby. People are funny about cancer. It still has such a stigma attached to it. Even well-meaning friends would not be able to behave with equanimity in Gabby's presence."

A few minutes later we tiptoed into your room. You were in an oxygen tent, still unconscious, lying pale and still, inaccessible to all but angels. They had unbraided your hair and it was lying tangled and damp about your face.

That was one of the most difficult moments of all for Daddy and me—to see you lying there, unknowing, trying so hard to breathe. How could we help you now, except to cradle you with love, knowing that never again could we be quite honest with you in the world's sense . . . maybe love would prove a greater truth than honesty.

The special nurse moved around the bed constantly, taking your pulse every few minutes, adjusting the rate of dripping in the infusion bottle, making notes in her chart. She was efficient and unsmiling. I was glad you couldn't see her. "The best nurse we have," they told us. Maybe, but two days later when you asked if you could hold her hand when they put in a needle, she said, "No, you might hurt me."

About noon you opened your eyes, and I got my head into the oxygen tent to kiss you. Daddy and I spent the rest of the day taking turns holding your hand. I begged to be allowed to sleep in your room that night. But it was impossible. The room was too small, they didn't have a bed—they had so many reasons.

The night nurse was large and rustly—a nylon uniform. She wheeled around the room making too much noise, I thought. "It's a shame," she said, looking at you, "and I've just come from the neurological. My patient died last night, a little girl with a brain tumor."

Next morning when we got back to the hospital, you were out of the oxygen tent. You were still very dopey but you did ask about the operation. "Everything went so well," I told you. "They found nothing at all. It really is only infectious hepatitis after all, but it is going to take you a long time to get completely well."

"Well, that's good," you murmured, shutting your eyes. The injections of Demerol helped with the pain, but it did hurt so to move and your arm had to be kept still and in the same position until Monday afternoon when they finally stopped the intravenous fluids.

We took the special nurses off on Tuesday and that was a relief, too, because, efficient as they may have been, they were by no means cheerful. The young floor nurses, in great contrast, were almost always cheerful and gay, and warm and loving, too.

Your operation had been a great shock to the hospital personnel. Dr. Heldt, the young resident doctor, had been transferred and I didn't see him for several days. When I did run into him, he admitted, with embarrassment, that he had been avoiding me.

"I was at the operation," he said, "and it was unbelievable. I've grown so fond of Gabby I don't know how to behave with her. She's so terribly bright—I think she knows more than all of us." (An opinion Dr. Lynde was to voice more than once in the weeks ahead.) "I know I shouldn't feel this way. It's one of my problems as a doctor. I get too involved with my patients."

And he never did come to see you again. You asked for him many times and I made up stories. He would send you messages with other doctors and he would promise to come whenever I met him in the hall or elevators. But he didn't.

When I came to the hospital on Tuesday, you had been moved. The nurses decided you should have a more cheerful room, so they had moved you into one of the rooms off the main corridor, nearer their desk. The room had two large windows facing east. All your plants and toys had been arranged around the room and it did look more cheerful. "And now we'll find you a roommate," they promised.

The next day they brought in Sara, a little blonde girl about six in a crib. It was fun for a while, but she was so much younger than you that she wasn't too much company. And when she wanted the nurse during the night she would wake you up instead of ringing her bell. But I guess it was nicer than being alone.

Things were quite gay that week. You seemed to recover from the operation so quickly—"because you were basically so healthy," the doctors said. Dr. Lynde had said maybe you would be able to go home for your birthday on the twelfth. In a few days you were in a wheel chair and could visit with Jill next door who had had her appendix out. She had a special nurse but you told her proudly, "My mother is my nurse."

There were ice-cream parties at night and much visiting back and forth. I remember one night in particular when you told Jill all about the hamsters you had in school and how one of them had died of a tumor. You described this in cheerful detail and Jill's nurse, who had heard about your operation, tried to catch my eye to express her amazement that you knew about tumors. You knew about lots of things.

Meantime, preliminary examinations showed definitely that the cancer was malignant, a rhabdomyosarcoma, and completely untreatable. The site of origin had not been determined; nor was it ever conclusively. Even though the doctors said it was hopeless, Daddy and I were determined to try to do something. But what?

I made an appointment to see another doctor at another hospital, a cancer specialist I had met up in Truro one summer. He didn't know you but he had heard about you from Sylvia and Bob. He gave me what turned out to be some very good advice. He said firmly that you were in the best possible hospital with the best possible doctors and that to travel around the country or the world trying to find something to help you would be futile, exhausting, nerve-racking, and unfair, besides being fabulously expensive.

It was hard for us to let go of the idea that somewhere, somehow, someone could be found who could do something. But we did stop searching in that way. Instead we substituted faith and began to live from day to day, knowing that each day might be the last for you, and therefore was a special day, full of significance, to be enjoyed completely.

You were always terribly good at living in the moment anyway, being about twice as alive as most people, even most children. Daddy and I were reminded of how often we used to speculate together, quite frivolously, about "how many days were left in the box" for each of us. Now we had an idea about how many you had left—not the exact number but too few to speculate about. We just decided to try to live them as fully as possible with you. I thought about how interested people always were in a baby's first days—last days shouldn't be any less important or interesting.

Dr. Lynde spoke to us about the possible use of mustard gas—triethylenemelamine. The results would be uncertain. In some cases tumors had been temporarily shrunk by this means, though there was little known about how it might act on a rhabdomyosarcoma. Also, the side effects were unpleasant and sometimes dangerous. It would probably increase your nausea and might depress your blood count. We decided against using it for the time being, because you seemed to be feeling so well.

The doctor said that you could definitely go home on Monday, just ten days after your operation, so that you would be at home for your tenth birthday on February twelfth.

I didn't tell you but I was concerned about how I would manage at home, especially if the bad pains were to come back. And that seemed to be something we had to expect. I talked to Miss Haeberle, one of your favorite nurses, and almost persuaded her to come home with us. But the hospital wouldn't hear of it. And it's just as well because we really didn't ever need a nurse. Instead I learned to give injections myself.

Miss Atkins, the head nurse, gave me a syringe and an intramuscular needle, and I practiced at home on an orange. The day you were leaving the hospital, she even let me give her an injection in the arm. I didn't tell you that I broke the needle doing it. But I wasn't really worried about this because I knew that if you really had bad pains, I'd certainly be able to give the injection properly. (And I did.)

Finally, Monday arrived. Before going to get you, Daddy and I went to the surgical supply store across the street from the hospital and bought some stainless steel emesis basins, a little bedpan, a covered dish for the syringes, tongs, sterile cotton pads. At the drugstore we had the prescription filled for Demerol and needles and syringes.

Meantime, at the hospital the doctor had removed your stitches and given them to you on a glass slide. So many of them. We took a big box into you, a pre-birthday present, the long-promised blue storm coat. I braided your hair into two pigtails, tied with red ribbons. You wore your brown jumper with the brown-and-white checked blouse.

There were good-bys to be said—little Julie in the next corridor, doctors, favorite nurses, and then, at last, we were on our way home. But that short trip to Fifty-seventh Street and the few steps going into the apartment building were exhausting for you. You could barely greet Nany and Deirdre and Cindy who barked and jumped all over you. With no prompting, you went immediately to your room and to bed and a few minutes later to sleep.

But not before expressing your delight at how we had fixed up your room. New sunny yellow calico curtains, little red cotton rugs on the floor and the furniture re-arranged according to a sketch you had made once, the main feature of which was a low counter with plants on it, separating your part of the room from Deirdre's. The counter was there and the plants and even a beautiful round goldfish bowl with two spry fish in it, though, for the time being, Deidre had moved into the little maid's room to make things quieter for you.

But you couldn't stay awake. Murmuring your approval, you went off to sleep happier than you had been in weeks.

The next day, February twelfth, was your birthday. We had our traditional early morning celebration all together on our big bed. The presents had been arranged on the little round white table the night before—the white, furry, almost real kitten, the ceramic kit, the Scrabble game and, best of all, the really magical little music box from Daddy. The Swiss chalet with stones on the roof to hold down the thatch and outside the door a well with a tiny pail. By lifting the roof, one could listen again and again to "The Bride of Appenzell."

Later on in the hospital after being unconscious for several days, you suddenly said, "The nurses didn't have the birthday party for me yesterday like they promised."

I explained that you had had your birthday party at home, but you couldn't remember it at all. Going to bed late that night I asked you if there was anything you wanted me to remember for you, and you wanted to hear about your birthday party.

I told you how you were propped up on the divan in the living room with the coffee table set with place cards for Nina and Marnie and Jean and Deirdre. The crepe-paper decorations were turquoise (your favorite color) and lavender and pink. No, you hadn't worn your new white party dress, your yellow print bathrobe had seemed more comfortable. We were to see movies but Daddy had trouble with the projector and it went off in the middle of a reel. But that didn't seem to matter, it was such fun to see Marnie and Nina and Jean again. During the festivities your teacher arrived with a big cardboard box full of presents from the children in your class.

But you couldn't remember any of these things. It was only when I told you that the music box was one of your birthday presents and lifted the little roof that you began to remember yourself. The little tinkling tune of "The Bride of Appenzell" seemed to waken some deeply buried memories and made you feel good.

During the party you seemed to have some tummy aches, but not really bad ones so that codeine tablets were enough to keep you comfortable. But you couldn't stay up very long at a stretch. You got so terribly tired.

The next morning, coming out into the hall and going around the corner toward the kitchen, you suddenly screamed, "The light! turn it off! It's too awful!" and I came rushing to you. I thought something had happened.

It seems strange now, but it was only the dingy hall light that upset you so much. The usual 100-watt bulb had burned out and we had had to put in a 40-watt bulb temporarily. It was a dim, depressing light, but your reaction was greatly out of proportion. But you became increasingly sensitive to all sights and sounds and smells, too.

The least noise would wake you from your sleep. So we had to make a rule that no one could even tiptoe in the back of the house when you were sleeping. Otherwise you would wake and be frantic—a feeling, I think, familiar only to people who know that their equilibrium is desperately dependent on sleep.

You said once, most sympathetically, "I know now how you used to feel when Deirdre and I were little and made so much noise on mornings when you needed to sleep."

The week went quickly. You were eating well and sleeping much. We talked about going back to school. You were still jaundiced and you said, "But I could wear yellow dresses and no one would notice." We made an appointment with your teacher to come and give you some special tutoring to catch up, but when the day came you didn't feel up to it.

Daddy and I made an arrangement to rent a movie projector for several months and then we tried to find suitable movies. But it was difficult to find good ones that we could rent cheaply. I phoned everyone we knew who had access to films and asked them to help. Everyone promised, but I couldn't explain why we needed them so badly and so quickly. We didn't know how much longer you'd be able to sit up and watch films.

Although you had never cared much for movies, you seemed to enjoy them now. And it was a good way for you to entertain other children. Although you wanted so much to see your school friends, you didn't have the strength to play with them. But during a movie you could have the feeling you were participating in fun with the other girls, and they didn't have much opportunity to see how yellow you were or how quickly you tired.

I remember one afternoon when Pamela was leaving,

you suddenly threw your arms around her at the door and said "I love you, Pam" with such intensity and fervor. Daddy and I knew then that we weren't exaggerating your need to see your friends.

You had a fairly good appetite and, although you slept a lot, you still enjoyed reading. You were anxious to use the new pottery kit you got for your birthday. The clay was the kind that can be baked at home in the oven.

We imagined a whole set of dishes but began by molding two little bowls. I spread the newspapers on the floor by your bed and we worked at it together, using two glass bowls from the dime store for molds. It was messy work to do in bed but so satisfying, somehow. The bowls turned out nicely and we set them aside to dry for a week before they could be baked. After the baking we applied the glazes. You chose a soft butter yellow for the inside of yours and a pale turquoise for the outside. The pattern of faint lines left on the clay by the cloth we tied it in seemed too pleasing to try to cover up, so you carefully filled in the lines on your bowl with pink, using a fine brush. It's a lovely bowl. I have it here on the desk.

Ten days after you left the hospital you were to return for a checkup. We all dreaded the visit. Although I had talked to the doctor several times on the phone, reporting that you felt quite well, he had warned that you might need a blood transfusion.

I think now you should never have made the trip uptown. It was too much for you—too much shaking up for your insides. I should have insisted on having you examined at home. But I never knew quite when I should insist about medical things.

On the day of the visit you got dressed in pale blue slacks and a blue angora sweater. You looked beautiful in spite of being pale and thin—thin, except for the area over your incision which now was beginning to look swollen. I saw you lift up your nighty one day at home in front of the door mirror and look rather wonderingly and critically at the strange incision, high and wide across the upper abdomen. Did you know I saw you? Later on I mentioned how swollen you seemed. We couldn't hide this from each other, and you said in an off-hand way that you supposed it was normal after an operation.

Dr. Lynde's offices were on the ground floor of the hospital. His examination was brief. He said you were doing well and then said that Dr. Ferrone, the surgeon, wanted to see you, too. The long trek over to the other end of the hospital was foolish. Daddy carried you most of the way but this wasn't really comfortable either. Why didn't we think of using a wheel chair?

And then you wanted to see your friends and nurses on the ninth floor. The nurses greeted you warmly. "May I see Julie?" you asked. "Oh, Julie's gone home," the nurse answered brightly. "We lost her," she whispered to me later. Julie had died a few days after you left the hospital.

You were exhausted when we finally got home. It was that evening, Thursday, just ten days after you left the hospital that you got your first really bad pain. You had been having pains of some kind every day, but usually they would go away quickly or be eased by codeine. You had had pains in your thighs, in your right leg, pleural pains that took away your breath, headaches, rectal pains. But this was different.

You had gone quickly to bed and to sleep when we got home from the hospital but you woke about six thirty with a headache. I gave you a codeine pill. But by eight o'clock the pains were so severe at the base of your spine and the backs of your legs that I decided to use the Demerol, 1 cc. of it. I had had the syringe and the tweezers and the needles sterilized and ready on a little tray ever since we left the hospital. You were wonderful.

Together we chose a place on your thigh and I did it quickly and somehow. You encouraged me so and told Daddy afterward that I was almost as good as the nurses, which wasn't quite true.

The Demerol made you feel good. Sometimes in the hospital it had made you very talkative. We had such good chats after Demerol injections. And you were very aware of the connection between the sense of well-being and the Demerol and confessed one day.

"I would just like to have an injection. It's so nice. But I don't think I really need it."

The next day, Friday, you awoke at nine and ate a good breakfast. You enjoyed breakfasts so much. I guess you really enjoyed all meals at home. You went back to sleep directly afterward and I prayed that the bad pains wouldn't come again. During the afternoon you complained of feeling stiff everywhere. But it wasn't until eight that evening that you got a really bad pain and this time in your tongue. There was no lesion in your tongue or face. Why the strange pain? I gave you codeine but by nine o'clock the pain was even more severe and now included the side of your face as well, so I gave you another injection of Demerol—1 cc. But half an hour later you were still in great pain, so I phoned Dr. Lynde and he said I should give you ½ cc. more of Demerol—another injection. This helped and at midnight with 60 mg. of phenobarbital you got off to sleep.

Saturday you slept until noon. After breakfast we finished glazing the bowls and you wandered around the house a little. You often asked me to hold your hands, as you stretched both arms behind you. It was easier for you to walk this way. You would lead me around behind you. In so many ways, altogether, you were truly leading me.

No really bad pains came again that day until midnight when you woke from your sleep because the backs of your legs and the base of your spine were hurting so.

Dr. Lynde wanted me to try again easing your pain with 1 cc. of Demerol before increasing the dosage. This time it worked.

Dr. Lynde explained that we must increase the dosage of drugs very carefully and slowly. The effectiveness of drugs wears off so that gradually the body demands increased dosages to do the same work. We were warned that we would probably have to change drugs from time to time. But always we had to have something in reserve to handle the pain.

On Sunday you woke about ten o'clock feeling good. "I'd like to go visiting," you said. "I'd love to go up to the Carson's and see Nina."

I didn't know whether you'd be able to make it but I said we'd try. Why not? But when I phoned Virginia she said at first, "Could you come up a little later?"

Later? Your periods of feeling good were so very short. I didn't know whether you'd ever feel like going upstairs again, ever. I guess I hesitated, and then Virginia said, "We're having breakfast, but do come now anyway."

It was a big adventure. I fixed your hair, tied ribbons in your pigtails, and you wore the yellow bathrobe. We went up in the elevator. Nina was so pleased to see you. It was the first time you had been upstairs since way before Christmas. I sat down in the dining room with Ben and Virginia for a cup of coffee. Nina was showing you some dolls she had made.

After a very few minutes of trying to chat casually, I missed your voice. Nina said you had gone to the bathroom. I found you there in agony. Bowel movements were beginning to be so painful. I don't know what I said to Virginia and Ben, but somehow I got you downstairs again quickly and into bed. The whole beautiful visit had only lasted about five minutes.

You went off to sleep and slept most of the day, waking only briefly now and then, once to eat an orange. You didn't have lunch or supper until ten at night. With phenobarbital you went to sleep again and during the night codeine took care of a little tummy ache.

On Monday you woke at ten feeling good again. You enjoyed your breakfast and at noon ate a chicken and lettuce sandwich, but by four o'clock the bad pains had arrived. This time 1 cc. of Demerol didn't help much and so, an hour later, I gave you ½ cc. more. But you were still uncomfortable and feverish and you were unable to use your bowels or void.

Dr. Lynde had suggested over the phone that perhaps you were becoming obstructed rectally. At the time of operation, the surgeon had seen an ulcerous mass in the rectal region but had been unable to reach it.

The Demerol didn't seem to help as much as it had before at all. At midnight I gave you 1½ cc. and you finally dozed off. The pains were severe again at five and I gave you 1½ cc. again but at five forty you were still in pain. I couldn't give you another injection for four hours, I knew. The pain was dulled a little but it was still there. At eight o'clock, after really only a three-hour interval I gave you 1½ cc. more and called the doctor. He said he would come. At twelve I gave you another 1½ cc. and this time it didn't help at all. I called the doctor frantically and he came at once.

When Dr. Lynde arrived, he said the effectiveness of the Demerol had obviously worn off and we would have to switch drugs—to morphine. But he didn't have any with him and, besides, he couldn't give it to you right after the Demerol.

It was impossible for the doctor to examine you while you were in such great pain, but he told Daddy and me that he felt you were probably completely obstructed and should be in the hospital. I hated to take you back there, but after twelve hours of trying so desperately to help you and failing so miserably, I felt he was right. But I said I must go with you and he agreed to that.

Then we had to tell you. The doctor wanted to do it himself. I don't know exactly what he said. I came into the room in time to hear you say, "If I go back to the hospital, I'll never eat a meal there." And you never did. I don't know how much was sheer psychological resistance to hospital food or a natural result of the goings-on in your body, but surely some of the time during the next two months you would have eaten if you had been at home.

I explained that I would sleep in a bed right next to you and do all the taking care of you myself. You finally agreed that you might be more comfortable in the hospital. You were really in too much pain to care.

Dr. Lynde phoned for an ambulance and called the hospital. We were to have a room on the same floor and right next door to the one we had left two weeks before. The doctor gave you an injection of some sedative in lieu of the morphine and I packed a bag for us.

The ambulance came promptly with two big burly attendants who just wanted to lift you onto the stretcher and carry you downstairs. But Daddy and I insisted that they take you down in the large back elevator. You were doubled up with pain and the jolting of going down the stairs would be impossible.

As the attendants came into your room, you screamed at them "Don't you dare touch me" and they stepped back. In spite of your helplessness or perhaps because of it, you seemed such a strong and formidable human being. Daddy and I bundled you with blankets and carefully eased you onto the stretcher. We knew that each slight movement increased your pain but yet we had to get you to the hospital. All the neighborhood boys were standing around on the sidewalk as we came down the steps.

And then finally we were going up Third Avenue. If only we could have gone on the highway instead of on the uneven brick of that street. You seemed to feel each brick as we went over it and there was nothing that Daddy and I could do to help.

Going up in the elevator at the hospital, you announced to the attendants that you were not going to get off the stretcher until you had had the morphine and it had begun to work. They were anxious to leave but the nurses on the ninth floor did respect your feelings and made them wait for their stretcher, grumbling, outside in the hall, until you felt quite ready to be transferred into bed, after the injection of morphine.

You knew most of the nurses on the floor and they were your friends, but with a strange perversity the head nurse assigned a new nurse to you on your first day. She explained it to me, "I feel mean not to give Gabby a nurse she knows, but I think it's good for her to get used to strange nurses and not too dependent on ones she knows."

But why should you have to get used to anything at this point, I wondered. But there were more important things to worry about and, besides, we wouldn't need nurses very much at all. There was a sign on our door saying DO NOT DISTURB EXCEPT AT REQUEST OF MOTHER for which we were both grateful.

When the young resident came in to examine you, you gave him a scathing look and said, "Every doctor in this hospital knows what's wrong with me. Why do you want to examine me?"

He was a new resident doctor who had never met you before. He was quite unprepared for your fearless candor. But he was pleasant and friendly and won your cooperation by explaining the routine nature of his examination.

When he had completed the examination, he talked to Dr. Lynde in the hall.

"I'd like to try to catheterize Gabby," he suggested.

"You can try," Dr. Lynde said, "but I don't think you'll succeed at it."

Dr. Lynde told Daddy and me that he thought you were completely obstructed and that it most probably would be just a matter of days before you died. That was preparing us. But we were to get used to hearing this and we learned not to be too impressed with these pronouncements. I think people die when they are ready to die. There is another kind of preparation, conscious or unconscious, which needs to be completed first.

To most everyone's surprise the young resident was able to insert the catheter and catheterize you. It made you feel a lot better. And when you needed catheterizing again the next day, it was decided to leave the catheter tube in place, so there would be a steady emptying of the bladder and no opportunity for pressure to form. The catheter tube needed irrigating twice a day and this became an interlude that we looked forward to. It was not at all unpleasant and it gave us a chance to chat with the nurses. Only once did the catheter stop up entirely. We had a few tense hours wondering whether the mass the doctor had felt was causing a complete urinary obstruction. But no, by removing the catheter and putting in a new one, everything went smoothly again.

Mineral oil enemas were ordered, and after several of these you began to have stools, too. You didn't have much control over this functioning, but we fixed you up with diapers and it didn't seem to bother you at all. And for me, it was like going through your baby days again— mineral oil, powder, fresh diapers—I loved taking care of you.

You really were much more comfortable in the hospital. It was easier to keep you propped up in bed in a comfortable position, and when the bad pains came you could have morphine. I was free of the anxiety of not being able to reach a doctor quickly enough in an emergency, and, besides, now we could be together all the time.

There was a regular single bed in your room for me. It was lower than your hospital bed, but at night I pushed my bed over next to yours and by propping my arm up on pillows, I could reach your hand and hold it as we both went to sleep. The doctor had given me Seconal tablets for sleeping, to make certain I would get some rest, but it seemed easy to sleep holding your hand. Whenever you stirred or were uncomfortable or wanted a drink, I knew immediately. And when you were fast asleep, I could sleep, and did.

You didn't die during the next few days as we had been prepared that you might, so you and I settled down to enjoy what we could about hospital life.

We brought some of your favorite books back to the hospital and Mary, your doll, and the white, furry kitten. In a stationery store near by I found some little Japanese paper parachutes dyed in clear beautiful colors. One was a deep purple fading into violet and tinged with soft pink on the edges. Another, with true bright blue edges, blended into a soft turquoise with a yellow center. We cut the parachute strings and spread out the circles. I Scotch-taped them to the walls and we had wonderful cloudbursts of color to feast our eyes upon.

"I'm all twisted up inside," you told me one day.

"Where?" I asked.

"I can tell when I breathe," you answered. "But it's nothing," you added casually and impatiently, changing the subject.

You seemed quite determined not to surrender yourself completely to all the goings-on inside you. "After all, it's only the body," we would agree. The real Gabby was as well and alive as ever. Perhaps even more so.

We decided that evenings were the very nicest times in the hospital, and we got into the habit of going to bed late. March was a stormy month and often at night the wind and rain lashed against our high window, making us feel especially cozy inside. You were always interested in knowing who the night nurse would be, which was a good excuse for staying up until twelve. And then, too, if you had a sedative or a pain medication at midnight, you could often sleep through the night, at least until early morning. Another medication at five or six would let you sleep until ten. We both hated all the hustle and bustle of morning in the hospital, and we managed to escape a lot of it by very often not stirring ourselves until nine or ten.

Daddy would come and visit in the evenings and sometimes even Deirdre was permitted to come and see you, too. "She kisses so gently," you said one night after Deirdre left.

Daddy came as early as he could and stayed with you for private chatting while I went downstairs to the lunchroom to eat. Sometimes Daddy would bring me a sandwich, but it didn't seem right to eat in your room when you weren't eating at all. You drank juices and lime soda and milk, but our day was never punctuated with anything like real meals. Once you said you'd like a certain kind of coffee roll with frosting, but when I found it in a delicatessen near by, you only ate a little piece of it. And it didn't stay down.

Evening was bath-time, too. We would have a long leisurely bath and, when your skin seemed dry, we had what we called a blue bath, using a deliciously scented blue body lotion instead of water. Very often the nurses weren't so busy in the evenings once they got the toddlers in bed. Sometimes a nurse would come in with a baby and give him his ten o'clock bottle in our room. You loved the babies. You had never paid much attention to infants, but you seemed to take a new interest in them in the hospital. Once a nurse let you hold one of the tiny ones.

All sorts of evening rituals grew up. We always watched for the 125th Street starlings, an enormous flock of birds which passed by our window on their way home every afternoon about six o'clock. They swept by in flocks of a hundred or so and it took at least half an hour for them all to pass by. We often speculated upon where they had been. They spent the day in the country evidently, but why did they come back at dusk to New York City?

After the starlings we watched for the lights of the city to appear. By pushing your bed over a little toward the windows, we had an excellent view of a panorama of lights that extended almost to La Guardia Airport. They flashed on in a crazy sequence as though timed by the elaborate cue sheet of some erratic stage manager. There was one very bright white light which flashed on and off and on and off with great decisiveness. It always startled you when it began.

Before we ever thought of going to sleep ourselves, we had to put the flowers to bed. This meant giving them all a last sniff, changing the water and putting them in the bathroom for the night. Sometimes you had a special flower for your pillow, a carnation, perhaps. We would put this into a Cellophane bag for the night as though it were some loved doll. I remember one particular bouquet of anemones. I think you had a separate relationship with each flower! They lasted so long and each night you observed what changes had taken place during the day. Anemones die so gracefully the change is hardly perceptible. They are one of the few flowers that look quite beautiful even when they are dead.

And then I would listen to your prayers. Calmly and serenely you would say the Lord's Prayer with wonderful concentration, as though each time you actually thought through the words. And then you would God bless everyone you knew and loved, and from there you would go on to God blessing sick children everywhere and the people who were trying to help you. And then you would express the hope that you would be strong and well. First, it was by your birthday, and then by Easter, and finally after Easter you would just say soon.

I asked you once where you had learned the Lord's Prayer. I didn't remember teaching it to you myself. You said you had learned it out of a book by reading it in the light from the hall after you had been put to bed. You had gone to Sunday school a few times but you didn't like it at all, and I never insisted that you continue.

But you, like all children, were a natural believer with an enormous faith in God and a deep confidence that you were fulfilling a fitting and proper place in the scheme of things. I guess it's only as we grow older and become paved with pride and knowledge that we lose our understanding and begin to doubt and forget the things that once we never questioned.

Once you asked me, without waiting for an answer, "What kind of prayers are best?—not those of a man who is being killed and just prays because of that!"

You weren't comfortable at all, lying down, so that you had been propped into a sitting position that first day and stayed that way for almost four weeks. The pains continued on and off so that you seemed to need some morphine every day, sometimes only once or twice in twenty-four hours, but sometimes it was necessary to give you continuous dosages. The doctor was very cautious with the morphine. You were to have just what you needed and no more. The result was that the dosage didn't always last for the four hours before it was permissible to give you another injection, and the last hour was very difficult. But you tried not to tell your pain.

You wouldn't mention it to Daddy, for instance, or Nany if she were sitting with you, and you wouldn't ask for a nurse. You would just wait stoically until I came back and then as soon as we were alone you'd say, "Oh, Mummy, I need a medication so badly." You seemed, somehow, ashamed of the pain and you couldn't bear to have anyone sympathize with you.

"I'll turn into a dope fiend," you said one day. "I shouldn't take all this morphine." And in spite of our reassurances you tried to resist it.

Your thighs were beginning to be black-and-blue and very sore and tender from so many injections. Besides the sedations and pain medications, you also had to have Vitamin K shots frequently, because blood tests showed that your blood was not clotting properly. These were in a series of two or three usually, and they seemed to sting afterward. There were penicillin shots, occasionally, and twice during the two months everyone on your floor was exposed to measles and you had to have gamma globulin.

You were getting so very thin it became more and more difficult to find places for the injections which wouldn't hurt too much. You were so reasonable about this that the nurses gave up a technique that I had seen them use often with other children, a way of inserting the needle so quickly and deftly that it was over before the children realized what had happened.

This might have been all right with younger children but you hated being treated pre-emptorily. And I formed a sort of buffer state. A nurse couldn't rush in and do anything to you without first encountering my inquiries.

You told me what a relief this was. You said that before your operation you used to wince whenever a nurse or doctor appeared in the doorway, wondering what they were going to do to you.

With injections, we let you decide where you wanted them. Your arms quickly became too thin to use. Considering them one day you said, "Oh, no, they're too wasted." Another time, referring to your body, you said with a shrug, "It's just a rotten piece of material."

You didn't like being injected in the buttocks so we usually ended up by alternating places on your thighs. One day the nice English woman resident doctor suggested that we use ethyl chloride to slightly anesthetize the spot before using the needle and this helped a lot. From then on, I would spray the spot with ethyl chloride and the nurse would inject the needle.

One night late, Miss Haeberle, one of your favorite nurses, came in with a medication just before she was to go off duty. You carefully selected the spot and I sprayed it, but, somehow, as the needle went in, it did hurt terribly and you cried, "Oh, Miss Haeberle, you hurt me."

Miss Haeberle had an odd reaction. She turned quickly without speaking and left the room as though she were angry. This upset you very much.

"I didn't mean to hurt her feelings, Mummy. Please go and apologize for me," you begged.

I felt I couldn't interrupt Miss Haeberle then, when I knew she had reports to give to the nurses coming on duty. We decided that she must be terribly tired, although even I found her behavior very puzzling. But I tried to explain it to you. "Patients must remember that nurses are sensitive human beings with real feelings," I reasoned with you, trying to think what to say next.

Just then the door opened and in came Miss Haeberle. Her eyes were red and tearful. "Oh, Gabby, I'm so sorry. I've been in the linen room crying. I didn't mean to hurt you. I don't like to hurt people when I do things for them."

"But Miss Haeberle, it wasn't your fault," you cried. "I'm sorry I complained."

Tears were brushed away and everyone felt much better.

I suppose it's difficult for a young nurse not to become emotionally involved with her patients and I suppose that's why they assigned new nurses to you so often. But from your point of view, it was good to know that some of the nurses seemed to care about you in more than an impersonal way. Though last days, these were days of your life and it was right that you should be involved with those about you.

Every morning a lab technician came in and took blood for blood tests. Usually the technician was a young girl but occasionally it was the young man whom we nicknamed the blond bombshell. He was a slight young man with a waving blond shock of hair who whizzed into the room with his tray. He never said much and was gone again as quickly as he came, after carefully and swiftly pricking the necessary fingers and filling his little glass tubes. The girl technician, in contrast, was always very talkative and never in a hurry, it seemed.

The reports were usually back on the spindle of the head nurse's desk by early afternoon, and every few days, it seemed, you needed a blood tranfusion. This was always a long, exhausting procedure, and there were so many.

To begin with, it wasn't always easy for the doctor to find veins, so there would often be several trys just to get the needle in and the transfusion set up. After watching this for several weeks, I began to wish they would let me do this part. I felt certain I could do it more quickly and deftly, if they would just let me try. I couldn't bear your being so patient and brave, and the resident doctor not succeeding the first time. I wonder now whether I could have done it at all.

One day when the doctor was being quite unsuccessful jabbing you again and again to no avail, I said, quite without thinking, "Gabby, why don't you just leave your body for a few minutes, until the needle is in."

Dr. Gow, God bless her, quickly supported me. "I always do that in the dentist chair, Gabby," she said. "I just relax my body and leave for a few minutes and it doesn't hurt half so much."

"But, Mummy, I want to stay with you," you said.

"But I'm always with you," I explained, and you seemed to understand.

And it did seem to help you very much. It was a technique you were able to use more and more. Or perhaps pain itself is a means by which our consciousness is expanded, exercising against our will, like a long disused muscle, our comings and goings.

Once the transfusion was set up, the blood would take from three and a half to five hours to run depending on the difficulties we encountered. I don't think it ever went smoothly. It was necessary that it drip at a regular pace, neither too fast or too slow. But often it stopped altogether and then it was necessary to change the needle or the syringe or the whole assembly. Sometimes just manipulating the plastic tube with the fingers would increase the suction enough to get it going again. Or sometimes shaking the bottle would help. Sometimes you would fall asleep and move your arm and the needle would jerk out altogether.

And we never found anything very interesting to do during a blood transfusion. Sometimes I would read to you, short things like poetry, but we always had to keep one eye on the bottle. So, mostly, we just waited for it to be over.

We kept a fluid chart and you were very good about

drinking as much as possible but, sometimes, with all the vomiting, you got dehydrated and then it was necessary to give you fluids, usually glucose and water, intravenously.

But you weren't given any sort of consistent intravenous feeding. I asked Dr. Lynde about this one day and persuaded him to give you intravenously some Amigen, a protein liquid food. But he said that if he fed you properly, intravenously, you would have had a needle in your arm most of the time and you wouldn't have been able to enjoy anything at all.

And there were things you enjoyed, quite a few. Books, for instance. For a while you were able to read to yourself and later on, when you didn't have the strength for it, I would read to you. About this time, you said you'd "lost your taste for mysteries!" those endless series of Beverly Grays, Penny Parkers, Carolyn Keenes. You liked very much a biography of Robert Bruce and you enjoyed Eleanor Farjeon's beautifully illustrated *Ten Saints*. In a little book shop near the hospital, I found a great many Louisa May Alcott books. Of course, you knew *Little Women* and *Little Men* but now you read *Rose in Bloom*, *Jo's Boys*, *Under the Lilacs*, and even a book of Alcott short stories, *A Garland for Girls*. These last were gentle Victorian tales but they seemed to please you and I was grateful for them. In a short story called "Pansies" you read about the beautiful and serene widow Lucretia who "died at dawn on Easter morning after a quiet night." I was to remember this a few weeks later.

One evening Dr. Gow, the English resident doctor assigned to our floor, brought in her treasured picture book of England, and we had fun looking at the lovely photographs of English landscapes while she identified them for us. Dr. Gow had so many funny stories to tell about her life on a small English farm during the war. Later on that week, Daddy brought the movie projector to the hospital and we showed several films in your bedroom, including a travelogue of England and Holland to which we invited Dr. Gow.

But you tired quickly, watching the movies, and we only did it one other time. Daddy said he could get a film of *Little Men* and you said you'd love to see it. So, one evening we invited several other children and we saw the film, projected on the wall of your room.

Such a strange thing happened. The little boy who is going to die sits in a window, looking out at the other children playing, through most of the film. Whenever the rest of the boys talk to him they always say, "Be a brave little soldier." And when he finally does die, Jo says, "He was a brave little soldier." The morning after the night Daddy had shown the film, you received a handkerchief in the mail from a friend of Mummy's in New Jersey. It had red soldiers marching around the border and in blue lettering it said, "Be a brave little soldier." You quickly put it aside without any comment.

Although you had been vomiting several times a day all along, suddenly, during the third week in March you began vomiting much more than usual. And then what an elaborate game we played with each other to explain away the vomiting! Perhaps it was because you had drunk your milk too fast or too slow or too soon after juice. Then we would stop juice and milk and drink only lime soda or Seven-Up. When the vomitus was bloody, as it was so much of the time, we explained it away by calling it coffee grounds if it was dark enough. It was a term we had heard a nurse use in describing it. We didn't inquire too closely into what it meant. If it was too bright red to be coffee grounds, we would relate it to a nosebleed (you had them occasionally) or in some mysterious way to the transfusions.

When the vomiting got to be too frequent for us to try to explain, fourteen times in one day, for instance, we just gave up and agreed that anything that wanted to come up so badly just ought to and good riddance.

You were quite as good at this game as I was. I don't remember your ever asking me why you vomited so much. You always explained it to me, dismissing it as an annoying though unimportant nuisance.

Once, for several days, I noticed something that looked like tissue in the emesis basin. I had wild hopes that somehow the blood supply to the tumor had been cut off and that the tumor was gradually disintegrating, sloughing off its dead tissue. This was not beyond possibility, I knew, and the doctor agreed, though it was highly unlikely in a tumor as widespread as yours. We had the tissue sent down to the laboratory for analysis.

It was a long time before we got back a report saying that it was tissue of some kind but they were unable to identify it. And by this time you had stopped vomiting so much and there was no further sign of tissue being discarded.

There were so many things that the doctors couldn't explain. As your symptoms shifted and changed from day to day, the doctors could only guess at what might be going on inside you.

"We don't know what the course of the disease will be," they said over and over again. I remember Dr. Lynde standing at the elevators one day after his afternoon call saying, "Gabby probably knows more about this than all of us."

On the morning of Thursday, March 27, you quite suddenly seemed to feel much worse than usual in every way. You became increasingly restless and incoherent as the day wore on until by early evening you had slipped into a state of delirium. You became more and more impulsive and violent in your movements. We had to discontinue the blood transfusion which was in progress because it was impossible to keep the syringe in place. And by nine o'clock you were in a state of wild and voluble excitement.

Since your readmittance to the hospital on February 26, you had had your bed rolled up so that you were almost in a sitting position day and night. It hurt too much to lie down and you moved from side to side with difficulty. But now, in your delirium, you moved completely freely, throwing yourself about in bed with abandon.

We quickly put sides up on your bed and padded it all the way around with pillows so that you wouldn't hurt yourself. You kept trying to climb over the sides. After being so weak, you suddenly had amazing strength; we could hardly restrain you.

With your eyes wide open you flung yourself about yelling and shouting at the ceiling as though you were battling single-handed a host of demon adversaries we could not see. Where were your aches and pains and the stiffness now? With a look of terror on your face, you fought boldly and freely and definitely with the same frail little body that had hardly been able to move for weeks. How we wished we knew what those terrors were and how we wished we could have faced them for you. But Daddy and I and the nurses and the doctors could do nothing to help you. You were alone now in a realm we could not enter.

Once you asked me for a drink of water. You drank a little and I continued to hold the glass for you. You motioned for me to go away.

"I don't need any more," you said.

"You don't need what any more?" I asked.

"I don't need you any more, for anything," you said, triumphantly.

I took the glass away. What was this strange country you had entered where you didn't need me any more?

Whatever went on during that long and violent night, whatever the exact nature of your encounter, I am certain you vanquished your enemies. Your triumph was unmistakable. And then, gradually, after almost twelve hours of struggling, you eased into quiet unconsciousness, a well-earned rest.

You lay peaceful and still now, flat on your back for the first time in four weeks. Dr. Lynde told Daddy and me that we could expect you to slip away at any time, that you would most probably die sometime during the weekend.

We felt that we ought to prepare Deirdre. She had been spending the weekend in the country with Robbie. We phoned and asked that she be brought in to the hospital.

I met her downstairs but before we got into the elevators to come and see you, I took her into the waiting room which was fortunately empty and explained how sick you were, and then I added, "The doctors even think Gabby might die."

With a sudden rush of tears, Deirdre fell on the floor and began to sob uncontrollably. "It couldn't be true, Mummy," she said over and over again. "Doctors don't know everything. I know it won't be true. It can't be."

I agreed with her that doctors don't know everything, that nothing in life is completely certain. A few minutes later we tiptoed into your room. But you were far off now and didn't know that Deirdre had come.

She followed me out into the hall and said, with a trust that amazed me, "But, Mummy, God must have a reason."

Daddy stayed at the hospital with me through that night and the next. But you had no dream of dying or perhaps only a dream. Your body was naturally exhausted from the great exertion, but your breathing and pulse were steady and on Saturday about noon you seemed to be conscious of pain and we gave you some morphine.

It was late Sunday night before you regained consciousness and even then you were still too worn out to say much. But on Monday morning you woke with a smile and said, "I'm hungry. What happened to me anyway?"

What had happened to you? No one really knew but you were feeling better than you had been in weeks. How eagerly I prepared that oatmeal feast for you. Except for one egg and one orange and the coffee roll, none of which stayed down, the oatmeal was the first thing you had eaten since February 25. It was babies' strained oatmeal and you only ate two tablespoons of it but it stayed down and you enjoyed it enormously.

Dr. Lynde was unable to explain why you felt so much better and why you had not died during the weekend. But we didn't probe for explanations. We just delighted in our days together again, not knowing how many more there would be.

During the next week a friend came to see me at the hospital with the suggestion that you be placed under treatment with a psychic healing group—a few dedicated people, religiously unaffiliated, refusing money, who were loosely organized to try and treat illness by directing psychic energy. It would not be necessary for them to see you.

Although I had never heard of such a group, it didn't seem entirely unreasonable to me. Human beings are full of vital forces and energies that we know little about. Why couldn't these be channelized toward revitalizing debilitated bodies? I was skeptical of the stories of complete cures by this means, but perhaps it would be possible for skilled people to direct some restorative energies in your direction. Even if they could help with the pain.

So, without the need for active participation of any kind on our part, you were put under treatment. There were three treatments a day and I do believe they helped. After a while I told you about this healing group and it didn't seem strange at all to you and you added them to the list of people you blessed in your prayers. I will always be grateful to this group of people who were strangers to me for the modest, unselfish, and impersonal way in which they offered their help.

There were others, too, individuals here and there who helped to strengthen us with their thoughts and love, transmitting stations from God, I suppose. I certainly knew always, as I know you knew, that we were not alone through all these unusual and difficult days. We were surrounded and supported with love.

You continued to feel a little better, but only by comparison. You were still sleeping or dozing a good deal of the time. There was rarely a day when at some point your body didn't stiffen into unbearable pain, requiring morphine. You were still vomiting frequently. You were often feverish and blood transfusions were commonplace. The skin at the base of your spine had "broken down," a hospital phrase for a large, open bedsore which wouldn't heal, and required constant treatment.

But, in spite of all this, there were short spaces of time here and there through the days when you were very aware of life and eager to live it.

You continued to eat a few spoonfuls of oatmeal every day. Once you even ate a graham cracker. But oatmeal now seemed the greatest delicacy and these tiny meals were real occasions.

When Eric asked you to name a subject for a pen-and-brush drawing he had promised you, you suggested "An Oatmeal Feast on the Beach at Truro." When it arrived, to your utter delight, it was a picture of you, a terribly

shy and polite seahorse, and a cricket feasting on oatmeal in an overlarge sea shell dining room, discreetly
shaded from the rest of the beach by a piece of fish net.

By detaching the catheter tube and tucking an emesis
basin into your wheel-chair blanket for emergencies, I
was able to take you on short, if perilous, excursions out
to the sunny ward at the end of the hall or into the next
corridor. Once we even went up to the top floor by elevator and got a breath of very fresh air by opening the
door to the roof play space. We explored the craft room
with its tempting materials and you found a book that
looked interesting on a shelf in the playroom. But a trip
like this was exhausting and could never last more than a
few minutes.

On one of these infrequent adventures, you met a new
friend. Wanda was a little girl just your age who had
been hospitalized for observation but was not confined
to her bed. You were delighted with the idea of a new
friend, but Wanda's enthusiasms were mixed. She liked
talking to you, but she was a little leery of the goings-on
in your room.

She remembered the time that you were unconscious
for three days when your door was always closed. She
knew that you got frequent blood transfusions and, being ambulatory, she had seen your name on the critical
list at the nurses' desk. Besides, you didn't look as though
you were getting any better.

You were very, very thin now and, being jaundiced,
you were still quite yellow. Your long braids were often
untidy, though I tried to keep them tied with ribbons.
But I couldn't bear to completely comb your hair every
day because I knew how uncomfortable it was for you.
I gave you a dry shampoo once and the nurses suggested
washing your hair from a stretcher, but this didn't ap-
peal to either of us. When your nighty was pulled up, it

was shocking to see your spindly little legs and thighs, black-and-blue from injections.

Wanda had observed all this and it alarmed her. She was filled with fears about her own undiagnosed condition, and seeing you so sick didn't reassure her. Fortunately, she left the hospital before you did.

But you loved the idea of having Wanda to do things with, so I tried to keep you covered up a little when Wanda was around. You had three soft challis nightgowns, pink, yellow, and blue, sprigged with tiny flowers. They had long sleeves and high round collars. All covered up like that, with just your big blue eyes smiling out, you looked adorable. Your eyes seemed to get more and more beautiful as your little body dwindled away.

We had a small domestic crisis one night when you lost your kitten. We were getting ready for bed when we noticed it was missing. It was made of white bunny fur and had been your constant companion since your birthday. It had a pink ribbon around its neck now and two little cloverleaf good-luck pins Nina had sent and it was very important to you.

How we looked for it. Finally, we decided it must have been picked up with the sheets when your bed was made that afternoon.

I hurried out to the utility room and began pulling sheets out of the bin. White sheets, white kitten, I was afraid we wouldn't find it. The nurses sitting properly at their desks watched me tolerantly. It must have been against the rules for visiting mothers to ransack the soiled linen or maybe that situation had never arisen before. But I'm sure they were as pleased as I was when I found the kitten and could bring it back to you. I didn't want you to have even small disappointments. They could seem very large in our days.

You had many dreams which, maybe foolishly, I

copied down as you told them to me. Did I hope that I would someday be able to decipher the cryptic language, break through your words and phrases into an illuminated area where all would be clear to me at last?

One night after we had both fallen asleep, you woke suddenly and began to speak very clearly.

"Do you really want to know what's going on?" you said.

"Of course, Gabby," I said, quickly getting to the bathroom door and opening it, which let in a shaft of light.

"Well," you replied, very seriously, "all the Japanese people wanting to be helped from hurting, so—" and your voice dwindled off.

"What do you mean?" I asked.

"Oh, it's too complicated," you murmured, slipping back into your dream.

Once in the morning when you woke, you said, "I dreamed or imagined that each galaxy of stars was a finger of God or a part of him—and there were so many." I didn't even know that you knew the word "galaxy."

Another time you said, "I was in the manger or stable with the Christ Child. I was one of the shepherds or something. The Wise Men ate with the plates and then banged them up. I thought they must be freaks or something but I respected them too much to say so. I was scraping the plates but then the plaster began to come off and it began to get rough and I tried to smooth it."

As you told me your dreams, I often thought of a crayon drawing you had done when you were eight, a complicated, intricate pattern which you had entitled "A Lady Having a Dream of Herself in a Design." Is that what you were doing in your dreams, trying to imagine yourself into the scheme of things?

Some of the evenings now were beginning to be balmy and springlike. The night air coming in our window was gentle, filled with promises, and we occasionally felt lighthearted in spite of everything.

One evening, it must have been in early April, when we turned out the light and put up the window shade, the full moon shone into our room with a radiance and light that was startling.

"It's looking right at me," you said. "I think it's a good omen!" But, without noticing it, you had mispronounced the last word, saying "amen" instead.

Often as I walked on the sidewalks outside the hospital these days, coming back with a bunch of violets for you, or a new game, or something to make, I would experience the exhilaration that comes with a heightened sense of life, not death. Coming back into your room I was always conscious of the small miracle that you were still alive. There you were. I could touch you, kiss your forehead, tell my love. Besides, I felt that there was a special quality of light and lightness around you. Many things were painful, but the atmosphere was never gloomy.

It wasn't only I who noticed the special atmosphere of your room. Doctors commented about it, as did the nurses, and even the cleaning woman said she loved to come in to clean. If you were awake at all, you had a smile for her and she would linger with her mop and pail as if reluctant to leave your company.

And how you guided me, like a gentle but firm little shepherdess. I was not permitted to feel sorry for myself.

One night late as we were preparing for bed, you said, quite unexpectedly, "You looked worried today."

"Did I?" I replied guiltily, turning away.

"Yes, and I don't like that," you said, almost sternly. "I expect you to be able to go through all these things without breaking down."

"Without breaking down," what a grown-up phrase.

I felt as though a steady hand had been placed on my shoulder.

"But, Gabby," I mumbled, "of course I'm not going to break down, just as I know you're not. It's a nice thing we can know about each other." And the moment was quickly gone, you were your little-girl self again.

You never cried or felt sorry for yourself and you didn't like expressions of sympathy from others. In spite of all the things happening to your body, the buoyancy of your spirit seemed always to maintain itself, and me.

By THE THIRD of April you had stopped vomiting altogether and you didn't vomit again for ten days. Your need for morphine diminished, too. It's true that you began to run a high temperature instead, and you complained of headaches, but these symptoms did not bother you as much as the constant vomiting.

Several times Dr. Lynde had spoken to me about my staying so long in the hospital. He had asked me if I thought it was really necessary and whether it was really fair to Daddy and Deirdre. I always said yes and he didn't press the issue.

But now that you were feeling a little better, he took me into the visitors' room one morning to try and persuade me to leave the hospital.

"Gabby may be here for months," he said, "it's completely uncertain. We don't know what path the disease will take. Your room is so expensive. Is it fair to the rest of the family to pile up such a debt?" he asked me. "Don't you think Deirdre needs you at home?"

These were difficult questions to answer. I knew that

the responsibility of a doctor caring for any cancer patient must include the patient's family. Cancer can be completely crippling financially as well as emotionally, as it runs its drawn-out and erratic course. I knew all this and appreciated what Dr. Lynde was trying to do.

On the other hand, how could I make up my mind to leave you. I often had supper with Deirdre in the hospital cafeteria and I thought I knew how she felt. With her imaginative understanding and truly generous nature, I knew she wouldn't want to feel that she was responsible for your being left alone nights in the hospital. That I should stay with you when you were sick, just as I would stay with her if she were sick, was something that Deirdre seemed to understand and accept.

Finances were another matter. We were fortunate in having been able to borrow money, but, of course, I could not continue to stay with you indefinitely.

"But Gabby will never be able to go to college. We'll spend that money now," I parried the doctor. But we both knew that even the money for a complete college education would be expended in a few months in the hospital, if I continued to stay with you.

So, I agreed, at last, and thanked the doctor, but I still managed to avoid setting an actual date for leaving the hospital. "After Easter," I said vaguely.

I discussed it with you. "It costs so much money, much more than we have," I explained. "I may have to move out of the hospital after Easter. They'll move you into a room by the nurses' desk."

"But, of course, Mummy," you responded so quickly. "You can't spend so much money. I'll be fine by myself at night."

And I'm sure you would have been, one way or another, but how would I be able to sleep at home knowing how often you waked in the night? And if I became worn out with fatigue how would I be able to take care of you at all?

Special nurses were expensive, too, and the only time we had hired a special nurse for one night's duty was not a happy experience. She arrived at midnight with a good book and insisted on sitting with the bathroom door open so she could read by its light, even though the light then shone directly on your face. You couldn't fall asleep that way and I couldn't persuade her to move or give up the book. I was too exhausted to argue and finally fell off to sleep myself, but we were most happy to have her leave at seven. I took better care of myself after that and we never had to get another special nurse.

My secret hope was that your symptoms would some-how regress and you could come home again. I dreamed of taking you to our hilltop in Truro in June and flying you to a hospital in Boston if you became suddenly ill. But I didn't mention this to you or the doctors because it was out of the question at the moment. With the con-stant blood transfusions and intravenous feedings and tricky pain medications, it would have been silly to leave the hospital. You seemed to realize this and never asked directly about going home any more.

You had stopped talking about school, too, though I guess you thought more about it than we knew. I re-member one morning when your eyes filled with tears as you looked at a letter you had received. The envelope was addressed in very careful penmanship.

"It's from Jean," you said. "They're learning con-nected writing. I'm missing it."

Now that the vomiting had stopped, Dr. Lynde and Daddy and I again talked about using triethylenemela-mine. Although in some cases it had been known to shrink tumors, its use was hazardous, we knew. There was no way of predicting results. In the few cases in which it had been tried, some patients had become much sicker, and there was nothing known about how it might act on your type of cancer, a rhabdomyosarcoma.

Although Dr. Lynde did obtain some of the drug in usable form, we decided to postpone using it. When you were feeling very sick it had seemed too risky, and now that you were feeling relatively better we didn't want to make you feel worse. And so, in fact, we never did find a time which seemed completely propitious to experiment with triethylenemelamine.

EASTER was only a week away. Your temperature was high most of the time now and antibiotics didn't seem to help. I bathed your arms and legs frequently with cool water, but any relief was temporary. Even so, in spite of the continuing high fever, you were looking forward to Easter festivities.

You and Wanda planned to make Easter baskets and fill them for the younger children in the wards. I found some cardboard cutout baskets that were easy to make in bed and I bought all sorts of Easter confections—sugar eggs with magical scenes inside, marzipan fruits and vegetables, tiny chocolate eggs covered with tinfoil. You delighted in examining these, though you were not at all tempted to taste them, and then we put them away until Easter Eve when you planned to fill the baskets.

You were drowsy and apathetic much of the time but I noticed that when the idea of making something really stimulated your imagination, you seemed to be supplied somehow with an extra spurt of energy for its accomplishment. You were able to spend several hours, for instance, making charm bracelets for Deirdre and Nina for Easter presents. You made a rather complicated Easter Card for Nina in the form of an egg with a hidden envelope for a message, and you wrote Nina a letter.

But the activity you enjoyed most was coloring Easter eggs. I'm afraid I let you keep at it much too long. I knew you were expending your little strength extravagantly, but I hadn't the heart to stop you because you were having such a thoroughly good time.

Eric came for the occasion and Nany boiled the eggs for us at home ahead of time, although we found out later that the hospital had also provided eggs for coloring. The nurses found us a long, narrow, chromium utility table and we wheeled this into your room, putting it lengthwise beside your bed. After covering it with newspapers, we set out our materials. Such a collection. Besides the many cups of dyes we had gold paint and brushes and sequins and glossy colored papers of all kinds.

You were bubbling over with ideas about how to decorate the eggs. You thought of dyeing small squares of bandages, for instance, letting them dry, and then pulling them tightly around eggs of a contrasting color. With sequins underneath, they looked like mermaids' Easter eggs, tied with frail fish net.

After Eric left, you and I kept at it alone and when Daddy came and I had to leave for a while, you insisted that Daddy share in the fun of egg-dyeing with you. This was much too exhausting and perhaps I should have stopped it, but what better way to spend time than in making something beautiful. And they were beautiful! We arranged them on Easter grass in a big box and nurses and doctors from all over the hospital dropped in to see them. I suppose it's silly, but I still have them wrapped individually in aluminum paper in a box on a shelf with the Christmas tree decorations.

There was a new young nurse assigned to our floor that week. She took a special interest in you and spent a good deal of time in our room getting acquainted. She enjoyed particularly telling us about roller-skating derbys.

You listened with some interest to her enthusiastic descriptions of gangs of girls racing around the rink in stiff competition. But to both you and me it seemed like such an improbable sport because neither of us had ever been much good on roller skates. One morning when she came on duty, she brought you a program from the session she had attended the night before and a pair of miniature roller skates.

"If you could just see it on television," she told you. "Maybe I can rent a television set for you for Saturday afternoon and you could see the exciting Saturday afternoon derby."

From her description of the violence and aggression, the drag-out fights between the girls on wheels, I decided that this would not be entertaining for you. Besides you disliked television. Several friends had asked if they couldn't have TV installed in your room for you but you were absolutely against it. You had always been much more interested in doing things yourself than watching other people have fun. And now you were far too ill and debilitated to be able to withstand the impact of even a noisy voice, let alone television.

Still, we didn't want to offend Miss Kenny with her generous offer to rent a TV set for you. "We'll see," I said, and I was most relieved when Saturday came around and Miss Kenny reported dolefully that she hadn't been able to get the set after all. I would never have permitted her to bring it into your room, in any case.

Saturday afternoon was a time I often left the hospital for a few hours. On this Saturday before Easter, I wanted to get some surprises for both you and Deirdre for the morning so I left the hospital about noon, leaving Daddy in charge. Your temperature was 101.2. You had had pains and the awful stiffening feeling you described so often, so you had been given some morphine at eleven o'clock. I didn't think of mentioning the roller-skating derby to Daddy, considering the matter settled.

But just before two, Miss Kenny came in and told Daddy she had arranged for your bed to be wheeled out to the sun porch, so you would get to see the roller-skating derby after all. And Daddy, thinking it was by some previous arrangement, gave his consent. So your bed was wheeled out and for an hour or so that afternoon you watched the mad violence going round and round on the television screen. When I returned to the hospital at five, your temperature was 103.2 and the bad pains had come again, so we gave you more morphine.

I felt uneasy about you because you seemed unusually keyed up. When I heard about your afternoon, I thought maybe the television was responsible for your feverish, excited condition. What we know now and didn't know then was that your fever was caused by a purulent infection of the central nervous system, involving the lining of the brain. No wonder you were restless.

You and Wanda filled the Easter baskets as you had arranged to do and then I tried to get you to settle down and sleep although it was only early evening.

But you were determined to stay awake until the nurse who was to distribute the baskets came for them. "I want to know the judgment of the baskets," you said. Such an odd phrase, and so unlike you.

Your temperature gradually dropped until it was down to 100 by eleven o'clock, but you still weren't ready to sleep. You were strangely excited and a little incoherent.

Partly dozing, you said, "I was having a vision of Nany telling you something in a dream—and the Resurrection." And then a few minutes later, "I dreamed that this was all a vision, very complicated."

At midnight I asked the nurse for some Luminal, thinking this might quiet you. I was anxious that you sleep well so that you would be able to enjoy the fun of Easter morning and the surprises of the Easter Bunny.

After the Luminal injection, we said our prayers and I turned out the light, hoping you would at last fall asleep. But, we had only been in bed a few minutes when you suddenly vomited, for the first time in twelve days.

I changed your nighty and your pillowcase and bathed your face with cool water. We tried to think of what could have made you vomit—our old game. Finally, we were about to settle down for the second time, when, just as suddenly, you vomited again.

I decided to take your temperature and found it was 102.8. You were very restless now.

"The call is coming, the call is coming," you sang out in a singsong way several times. You looked so very strange that, alarmed, I rang for the nurse. Just as she came to your bedside, you had your first convulsion.

"You had better step outside," the nurse said to me.

Step outside? What an impossible request. I assured the nurse that I wasn't frightened by convulsions and that I had no intention of leaving you at such a crucial moment.

The convulsion only lasted a minute or so and we fortunately had a tongue depressor handy and made sure that you didn't swallow your tongue. As the contractions subsided, we tried to get you to relax. But we were completely unsuccessful and twenty minutes later you had another seizure—a wave of spasms, shriveling your skin and distorting your face unbelievably. There was an interval of an hour before the next convulsion, but then the seizures began repeating every fifteen or twenty minutes.

The nurse called the resident on duty after the first convulsion and he in turn got in touch with Dr. Lynde who returned to the hospital. Daddy came back, too. But nothing the doctors tried seemed to have any effect on the relentless regularity of the seizures. We all stood around more or less helplessly watching you until by morning you had had twenty convulsions.

So many things went through my head. I thought of a little baby rabbit I had found in the woods once in Minnesota. I brought it home in my pocket, but the next day it became ill and cold. I took it out-of-doors and held it out to the full sunlight, thinking to warm it. But, as I held it, the baby rabbit suddenly had a convulsion and died in my hands. It was my only other experience with convulsions.

After each seizure your respirations were so depressed that we didn't know whether you would be able to catch your breath again. I remembered the Louisa May Alcott story we had read just a few weeks before in *A Garland for Girls* about the serene Lucretia who died at dawn on Easter morning.

But dawn came and you hadn't died. You were given some paraldehyde at eight o'clock which put you into a deep sleep and the convulsions stopped at last.

Your temperature rose steadily until by noon on Easter Sunday it was 104.4, indicating an acute infection which was obviously affecting the nervous system. The paraldehyde kept you deeply unconscious for three or four hours at a time, but we had to watch you carefully so that when you became restless again as it wore off we could give you more to prevent recurrence of the convulsions.

Penicillin had no effect on your fever, so on Monday, along with a blood transfusion and an intravenous feeding, you were given terramycin in solution, which we hoped would get at the infection.

In spite of all our precautions, you had another convulsion on Monday at six, another at eleven, another at three in the morning. You were vomiting again now, often blood, and there were other signs that you were bleeding internally.

How COULD so many things happen to one little body, particularly yours which was already so starved and ravaged? I thought of the time I met Dr. Ferrone, the surgeon, in the hall after your operation. "I hope something happens to her, a hemorrhage or something," he said. I thought he was being unnecessarily cruel, but he knew about the tortuously slow and painful disintegration of the body that often accompanies cancer. I could never have imagined it.

But I comforted myself that you, Gabby, seemed safely away somewhere else most of the time. Only occasionally did you wake up for a few minutes. You complained then of pains here and there, your right leg, your shoulder, a headache. Sometimes, quite incongruously, I thought, we gave you an aspirin for your headache and it seemed to help.

On Tuesday, after more penicillin, your temperature gradually began to subside. Although you had been given paraldehyde in the morning, this time as it wore off you seemed quite relaxed. And on Tuesday afternoon about three o'clock you woke up more completely than you had since before Easter and in an entirely different way.

You looked at us with a big smile. You looked around the room with interest as though you had been away on a long journey. You noticed your dolls and asked if you could play with Klumpe.

I didn't know whom you meant. You pointed to the Spanish boy doll made of felt that Paula had sent you. I had perched it on top of the dresser mirror so that he could look down at you and you could look up at him. I had never noticed before that the label sewed on his sleeve said Klumpe. For ten minutes or so you played with him before drifting off to sleep again.

Pains in your back and shoulder woke you in an hour or so, but after some morphine you fell asleep again, smiling. You had one more convulsion at six but by the next day your temperature was down to normal and you seemed to have passed through that particular dark valley.

On Wednesday you woke in the same amiable, docile mood. You didn't talk much but there was an air of quiet secrets about you. You were completely serene and, I thought, very indulgent with us, agreeing readily and nodding pleasantly in response to any and all suggestions. It was as though you knew something very special and wonderful and so could easily afford to humor us. As you smiled and listened politely to things that were said to you, I felt your thoughts were fixed on something else.

WE HAD discouraged visitors since our return to the hospital for many reasons. You were too sick most of the time to enjoy seeing people and the times when you felt well were completely unpredictable. Children were not allowed and there were not many adults whom you wanted to see.

I remember the time Bob came, though, at your special request. Daddy was there, too, that Sunday afternoon and I remember you weren't feeling very well when Bob finally arrived. But, nevertheless, you gathered your little strength and said, impulsively, as you looked at the three of us, "Couldn't we have some lemon-lime? Let's have drinks all around!" Who could resist such an invitation? So I prepared the drinks and we toasted you with lemon-lime.

Daddy came to the hospital every day and Nany when she could, though she was busy working and taking care of Deirdre. Outside of Eric and Helen, who supported us so beautifully, we had really no contact with the outside world.

But suddenly after Easter everyone we knew, it seemed, became alarmed. You had been sick too long and too mysteriously. People phoned me at the hospital. Others came to the hospital, wanting to see you. A group of mothers from your class came one morning full of questions and concern. I couldn't let them see you, but I talked with them, as casually as I could, in the visitors' room at the end of the corridor. When they left they gave me a get-well card for you and later, when we opened it, out fell three fifty-dollar bills.

Many people seemed to suspect the serious nature of your illness now. Among friends, a blood bank was organized for you; and people, some whom we didn't even know, came to the hospital and gave blood to make up for your many transfusions.

It was a busy time and I didn't handle it very well. It was difficult to talk with friends, and yet I didn't want to seem completely inaccessible to arouse their suspicions further. But I don't lie easily and they asked so many questions. Still, how could I tell the truth and listen to expressions of sympathy before you had even died?

Besides, they would never believe me if I told them that you and I were not afraid, that we had been having many wonderful times together and that it wasn't all gloom the way they were imagining it.

You were sleeping or dozing most of the time now, though occasionally you'd be awake for an hour or two. You didn't have the strength to do anything with your hands any more. You couldn't hold a book or even lift your head.

Once when I was turned away from you, you asked me sharply and impatiently, "Mummy, when will I be able to lift my head?"

I don't remember what I answered, but I didn't lie to you. I had tried that weeks earlier when, to give you some encouragement, I one day brought your new storm coat to the hospital and hung it up in your closet without saying a word. As I turned, you said gently and chidingly, "You know I'll never be able to walk out of here."

So now I didn't make promises. I told you things I believed to be true, that you were completely protected and sustained with love and that nothing bad could happen to you, the real Gabby, though how could I deny the devastation of your body? You were much too intelligent for that.

I think you and Dr. Lynde had a mutual respect for each other's integrity. He never gave you false hopes that you would be well soon, either. I asked him once if he could please say something encouraging to you. It was difficult for him. He knew that your almost clairvoyant intelligence would see through lies. But, I followed him into your room and he made a little noncommittal speech about ups and downs—you were having your downs and you would have your ups.

Sometimes now I wonder whether I should have told you the verdict of the doctors. But I don't think it would have made any difference. Death is implied and understood in living if you really live and we were certainly deeply immersed in that in our way. I think you understood.

One afternoon Eric and I were sitting quietly by your bed while Eric pasted pieces of colored gelatins he had brought from the theater onto a design of a stained-glass window cut out of cardboard. As he pasted each new color into the pattern, he would hold it up to the light for you to see.

It was a quiet activity and you seemed to be enjoying it very much, when, suddenly, you said to me, "Say, where are we anyway, in Truro or New York?"

"You're in New York," I replied with surprise, "in a hospital because you've been sick."

Although you had said earlier in the day, "I'm sort of delirious," I hadn't realized the extent of your disorientation.

You looked incredulous. "Did you have to buy a hospital?" you asked.

"No, you just rent a room in one," I explained.

At that you looked around the room with new interest and nodded approvingly. "You've fixed it up very nicely."

"Thank you," I said. It seemed like such an absurd conversation. "Where have you been anyway, Gabby," I said, laughing, "on a trip to the moon?"

You turned abruptly back to us and said with complete candor, "No, to God," as though you were explaining your absence at the neighbors or the corner drugstore.

You moved around in bed these days with great difficulty, but it was nevertheless necessary for you to change your position occasionally.

"If you don't move around," I told you one afternoon, "you'll get as stiff as an old woman."

"I am an old woman." You smiled back. "I'm infinity years old."

Although you could no longer read yourself, I sometimes read to you. Helen had sent me a book called *Winged Pharaoh*, a novel laid during the First Dynasty in ancient Egypt. The story began with a description of the childhood of a brother and sister who were to become joint rulers of the land. I thought you might be interested in this part of the book so I began reading it aloud to you.

You loved hearing about the fun Neyah and Sekeeta had growing up in the ancient temple with a lion cub and a baby cheetah for pets.

"Let's hear what's going on in the temple," you'd say, asking me to read.

I read stories about the many different kinds of lessons Neyah and Sekeeta had, lessons in spear-throwing, the flying of arrows, poem-making, writing on tablets of clay. I read about Sekeeta playing at being a dancing girl with her friend Neferteri and about trips to the marshes to watch the morning flight of birds and trips downriver where one could sometimes see gazelles.

You loved all this. I didn't find out until later that your fourth grade class was also learning about Egypt at the same time. Whenever I came to passages about battles or anything I thought might possibly disturb you, I skipped over it. But one day I found myself launched into a story that gave no hint of its ending until I had turned the page and then it was too late to stop.

An aged temple storyteller was sitting out on the grass telling old legends to anyone who would listen.

" 'There once was a man who walked upon stones until his bare feet bled,' " the story began. " 'He was offered sandals, but would not put them on.

'Then he found himself in a swift river and thought that he was drowning; but when strong hands would have pulled him into a boat, he tried to swim away from them.

'When he was sitting on a scorching rock at noonday, he saw before him cool trees beside a pool; and they invited him to rest in their shade, but he ran further into the desert. . . .

'When he was starving, a platter of his favourite food appeared before him; but he buried it in the ground and tried to stifle his hunger by licking a stone.

'And when the weather grew cold and he had only a few rags to hide his nakedness, they offered him fresh linen and a soft woollen cloak, but he would not wear them, and shivered in the storm.

'This story may seem hard to believe, yet if you think his foolishness passes understanding, do you not know one who is afraid to die? For if you do, you know one still more foolish than the man in this story I have just told you.' "

I quickly closed the book. I was embarrassed to have you think I would purposely make such secondhand and thinly disguised efforts to comfort you. But you covered my embarrassment.

"Do you think all that is true?" you said, casually and lightly, not really expecting an answer, as I put the book away.

But these reading periods could never last very long. Your attention span was growing shorter and shorter. Although you were not really unconscious, you seemed to be drifting and dreaming most of the time except when pain brought you sharply into awareness.

Blood tests were still taken regularly every morning and blood transfusions were necessary every few days. But one day when the results of the routine blood tests came back to the nurses' desk, your hemoglobin was up to thirteen.

"That's higher than mine," said a nurse standing by. "It must be a mistake in the lab," said Dr. Lynde, and another count was ordered.

But it was true. Your blood count was normal and no more transfusions were necessary. But it wasn't only your blood count that changed suddenly. Your sedimentation rate which had been high as it may be in cases of malignancy, up to seventy in your case, had dropped to three. The bilirubin count, showing the amount of bile in the blood, dropped, too. Dr. Klion, the liver specialist, came to visit you and reported that your liver was functioning better than it had since you were admitted to the hospital.

These developments were surprising to everyone. Daddy and I were so excited and hopeful. We thought perhaps some miracle had come to pass and you were going to stay with us after all. The doctors shook their heads. They were unable to explain it.

Dr. Lynde decided to remove the catheter which had been left in you all these weeks and we found that it was no longer necessary. You didn't seem to be obstructed at all. The swelling over your abdomen which we had assumed to be tumor mass was also shrinking. I measured it every day with a little ribbon, and I could see the difference.

Although all this clinical evidence seemed to indicate that your body was beginning to function more normally, you were more remote than ever. "I would believe that Gabby's condition was improving," Dr. Klion told me, "if I hadn't seen her."

I knew what she meant. You had little response when I told you what we thought was good news. And how could I deny the many other little signs—the hemorrhagic lesions appearing here and there on your hands and feet, the gently receding hairline back of your ears, the silvery pallor of your skin stretched smoothly over your face with all the fine bone structure showing. As you lay sleeping, your head flat upon the pillow, I thought I could sometimes see the unfamiliar but strangely beautiful mask of death already being tried on you.

Friday, April 25, was a quiet day and uneventful except that you ate two spoonfuls of cereal, the first since April 9. The bad pains came once about two in the afternoon and we gave you morphine. But most of the time you seemed to be fairly comfortable.

Late that night, after the lights were out, and we had settled down for sleeping, you added an afterthought to our goodnight chat. "Sweet dreams," you whispered, and these were, without warning, your last words for me.

Saturday was a dark day. Dr. Lynde arrived on his rounds at eight o'clock in the morning. I jumped up as he stepped into the room. "Go back to sleep," he said to me. "I'm just taking a peek at Gabby."

And I did go back to sleep. When I woke with a start an hour or so later, I found your eyes looking down at me, wide awake.

"Why didn't you wake me," I said, springing up. "And can't you say good morning to your mummy," I chided you, partly out of guilt for oversleeping. Before, I had always wakened first.

But you didn't answer. I let up the window shade. You always had some greeting for the day. "Good morning, day" or "Good morning, God" you were in the habit of saying as the shade went up, letting in the morning light. But this morning, not a word, nor did you smile. You only looked at me.

You had never been this unresponsive before except during periods when you were unconscious. I couldn't understand your behavior. As I changed your bed later with the nurses, I didn't seem to be able to handle you gently enough. Every movement made you wince. I felt I was of no use to you at all.

Looking back, I think you probably had a convulsion in those early-morning hours when I was asleep which would account for your inability to talk. You did not speak because you could not.

You fell asleep soon after we had changed your bed and were still asleep when Daddy arrived late in the morning. Because it was Saturday I had planned to be away from the hospital for a few hours while Daddy stayed with you. But now I feared that some slow change was taking place and I didn't want to leave. About noon, you had a mild sort of convulsion and then went off to sleep again. But Daddy said it was important for me to get away for a while and he finally persuaded me that I should keep my plans.

I did. I went to the theater and sat through the long,

tedious matinee of *Venus Observed*, not listening at all. My thoughts were with Deirdre. I felt, now, that all these months I had been neglecting her and so, as the curtain came down and before I jumped into a cab for the hospital, I went into a children's shop and bought Deirdre two red blouses. She's never worn either of them.

When I got back to the hospital, Daddy said there had been little change in your condition. You were still unresponsive and speechless, though you lay much of the time with your eyes wide open. But, oddly enough, you had eaten some cereal twice and even a little chicken broth.

For mothers, evidence of a hunger that one knows how to satisfy is always heart-warming. Preparing food for you was something I could do. All through that long night, at intervals, I gave you little spoonfuls of warm cereal and you ate it so eagerly as though you were genuinely hungry, or was it your way of communicating with me, receiving my love?

Dr. Lynde came in the early-morning hours on Sunday. It was obvious that you were in your third period of crisis. But you were not entirely unconscious this time. When I bent over and kissed your forehead, you always moved your lips in response. But you couldn't or didn't say a word.

I sat close by you all the morning, singing over and over again our old lullabys and favorite folk songs, and gently massaging your thin little thighs. About noon you became tense and restless and at one o'clock you had another convulsion. But you didn't have the strength for the violent spasms that swept you this time and when they finally subsided you could scarcely breathe. It was evident to everyone that you must surely be going to die now. Except Daddy and me. We tended to the moment and waited. You had passed through other crises.

At this moment, the doctors suggested to Daddy and me that we should leave you and wait outside in the room for visitors. Think of it, the greatest event of your life, and they wanted us to wait outside.

Daddy and I sat by your bed. He held his watch and I held your wrist, counting your pulse. I asked the nurse to bring in an oxygen tank and she did, to indulge me. She said it would do no good. Every once in a while I bent over to kiss your forehead and you always moved your lips in a kiss for me. Your respirations which had been weak ever since the convulsion gradually became slower and even weaker.

And then you didn't breathe for a whole minute and your pulse slowed down to almost nothing, too. Frantically, I tried to give you breath—carbon dioxide, Daddy said it was—and I immediately felt so silly. Whatever was going on was such a gentle, inevitable, peaceful process, I felt ashamed for trying to interfere with it.

But then you gradually began to breathe again—first twice a minute, and then three times a minute, and then every fifteen seconds. Your pulse picked up, too. A moment later, though, I noticed that you weren't breathing at all. I looked at Daddy and then we knew and then your pulse stopped and you really weren't there any more.

But you seemed to be in the room. I felt that you had been watching over and round us for several hours and that you had stayed connected with your body by some tenuous thread during this time only to help us and to make your sign of love upon the air up to the very last minutes.

As Daddy and I gathered your things together, at least six nurses rustled into the room like overzealous animated scene-changers and began to perform their various duties. I glanced at Miss Reynolds, released into activity, so busy and so sure of herself in the room of death, and then

I looked over at your frail little empty body. But only once. You were no longer there.

As we went toward the elevators wheeling a baby carriage piled high with books, dolls, toys, two suitcases, and no baby, we met Dr. Lynde who had tended you so devotedly for so long. We thanked him as best we could. We said we thought there ought to be an autopsy and he said he was just going to ask our permission.

We didn't get the report until late August and it was quite fantastic.

"The post-mortem examination, as well as the biopsy taken at the time of exploratory operation, showed a tumor composed of immature cells, some of which had differentiated into forms with cross striations, indicating that the tumor arose from muscle tissue. Therefore, it may be considered a rhabdomyosarcoma.

"The tumor was so widespread that the site of origin could not be determined. The largest mass was in the retroperitoneal region and involved the pancreas diffusely. The metastatic spread was found in many sites, including such unusual ones as the ovary and thyroid gland. In addition to these findings there was complete occlusion of the common bile duct with secondary cirrhosis of the liver. There was an infection in the portal vein ascending into the liver and a purulent infection involving the coverings of the brain and spinal cord. There were ulcers in the stomach and a terminal bronchial infection."

No wonder you had convulsions. The miracle is that you could live in such a broken-down house so long.

How could so many things go awry in a body that was as healthy and beautiful as yours to begin with? I know you were familiar with the struggle that science is waging with cancer from your reading, but what you didn't know is that cancer kills more children in the 5-15 age group than any other disease.

WE PICKED arbutus all morning on the day of your funeral. The shy, fragrant sprays were in hiding everywhere on the April hills, waiting to be discovered. I picked in all our favorite spots. Everyone helped. Even Jenny came from Bound Brook Island with Lisa and Daisy and Timothy and a big basketful they had picked in their woods. Together, then, we wove a blanket of arbutus for your small white coffin.

When we went to visit you the night before in the funeral parlor in Wellfleet, the whole place was overflowing with flowers. How did so many people hear the news so quickly? Deirdre was enchanted and couldn't stop smelling the flowers and exclaiming over the names on the cards.

Deirdre had suggested that Mary be buried with you because she was your favorite doll. You were all dressed up in the white Christmas party dress you had never worn before, but you didn't seem at all real. But Mary looked exactly like herself, still smiling, too.

For your burial place, Daddy and I had chosen a plot

on a hillside facing the bay in the old Snow Cemetery near Truro Town Hall where the square dances are held. (On the night of the first square dance in June all your friends trooped over to the cemetery to see your grave before the dancing began.) You would like the cemetery. Some of the graves are very old with poems engraved on the tombstones along with old-fashioned names like Thankful and Patience and Obediah. Very near your grave a girl is buried who died over a hundred years ago and now the same locust tree is shading you both.

It was a fresh April afternoon with a fine salty breeze blowing from the sea, making us look upward in spite of ourselves. We gathered on the hillside—Daddy and Nany and Deirdre and I, along with Marie and Stan and Peter and Connie and some of our neighbors.

The minister read the Twenty-third Psalm and then Eric read the poem on death from Gibran which begins:

> You would know the secret of death.
> But how shall you find it unless you seek it
>   in the heart of life?

It was a beautiful occasion, light and wondrous like you. But why am I telling you all this—you must have been there, as you are never far now. Otherwise, how would I have been able to walk away so flooded with the light of your strong and vibrant spirit, more able to live fully than ever before?